THE DYNAMICS OF
HARMONY
Principles & Practice

GEORGE PRATT

Open University Press

Milton Keynes : Philadelphia

Open University Press
12 Cofferidge Close, Stony Stratford, Milton Keynes MK11 1BY, England
and
242 Cherry Street, Philadelphia, PA 19106, USA

First published 1984

British Library Cataloguing in Publication Data

Pratt, George
    The dynamics of harmony.
    1. Harmony
    I. Title
    781.3   MT50

    ISBN 0-335-10595-5

Library of Congress Cataloging in Publication Data

Pratt, George, 1935—
    The dynamics of harmony.
    1. Harmony.   I. Title.
MT50.P913   1984   781.3   84-19000

Typeset by Gilbert Composing Services, Leighton Buzzard, Beds.

Printed in Great Britain by M. & A. Thomson Litho Limited, East Kilbride, Scotland.

Contents

Foreword

This book is a thoroughly considered reappraisal of the teaching of traditional harmony. The laboratory in which these methods have been tried and tested was the Music Department at Keele University, where I was Professor of Music from 1974 to 1984 and a colleague of the author. Although our new Department developed research interests and facilities in some novel areas such as American music, popular music, electronic studio and jazz, there was never any question of dispensing with the study of the materials of Western music and its heritage of masterpieces from the sixteenth to the twentieth centuries—in spite of John Cage's declaration that 'everything one needs to know about classical harmony can be taught in one half hour.'

Cage's exaggeration draws attention to the fact that there is now a vast amount of music outside the aegis of Western functional harmony and time is short, especially in joint-honours courses. George Pratt addresses himself to the task of getting the best results in the minimum time so that the technical elements can be effectively learnt from the start of the first year or before. He has never condoned the teaching of musical practice in the abstract, so the book is full of real music. I think he has been completely successful in his aims and I expect that at least a generation of teachers and students will be grateful to him.

Peter Dickinson

Acknowledgements

The stimulus to write this book has come from students whom I have taught, at Abingdon School and at Oxford in the 1960s, and at Keele University since. It was they who showed me that, while a vocabulary of vertical chords is normally acquired in preparation for school-leaving examinations, a feel for the tonal grammar and the melodic forces which guide their use is by no means so easily achieved. I then gained a great deal from discussions with Dr. Stephen Banfield, a colleague in the Music Department at Keele.

In particular I am indebted to the cohort of first-year undergraduates of 1983–4 at Keele who, with two of my colleagues to guide them, used a draft as a text-book. They were never slow to point out both grammatical infelicities and spelling mistakes (for which, of course, I always blamed my typing). More importantly, they considerably influenced the ordering of the material and the words in which I presented it.

Several individuals with markedly different academic and performing interests have also read the draft, in particular Professor John Paynter of York University, Janet Ritterman of Goldsmiths' College in the University of London, and my father, Ernest Pratt. Although I have benefited greatly from their suggestions and, above all, from their encouragement, I retain full responsibility for any errors of fact or judgment which may remain.

George Pratt
University of Keele
April 1984

Introduction

An understanding of harmonic processes is an invaluable aid to any musician, whether performer, listener or analyst, on several counts.

It creates, as do all kinds of familiarity with notation, a route to musical literacy and aural perception. Separate notes, like words, can be picked up off the page and 'understood' to some limited extent. But they can be grasped far more quickly and easily, and their deeper meaning seen more clearly, if they are read in groups, as elements in a wider grammatical construction.

Written music is hard to decipher silently through the eye and the imagining ear. We begin to learn it late; it requires extreme precision in perceiving pitch and rhythm compared with the needs of the written word; it involves retaining several symbols at once to assemble the composite sound of a single chord let alone the musical continuity of several harmonic progressions or the flow of contrapuntal lines. It is like reading several texts at once, an almost inconceivable challenge as far as written words are concerned. Any effective exercise in developing accuracy in reading this language of ours is beneficial.

A grasp of harmony is an essential tool for musical analysis. We can listen to music simply as sheer sound which washes over us, in one ear and out of the other, as we can listen to *Hamlet* translated into Serbo-Croat and enjoy the sound, with no understanding of it at all. But with analysis, not a dull examination-style dissection but a search for the processes, on the largest scale and in the smallest detail, which occupied the conscious or unconscious mind of the composer, we achieve an entirely different level of comprehension and appreciation. The sheer sound remains, but now enhanced by our grasp of the forces at play, of the tensions, the artistry and the overwhelming craftsmanship of an outstanding mind, long dead perhaps but reanimated by the performance of his music.

Harmonic usage is a salient part of most musical styles. Any historical assessment of a composer's music requires a recognition of the harmonic conventions familiar to him, how far they were adhered to, how far rejected or distorted. To make such judgments, an understanding of these conventions is indispensable.

What an understanding of harmony through writing imitatively will not do is make an original composer. There is little call for additional madrigals by Monteverdi or string quartets by Shostakovich, and if we wrote them they would probably be second-rate, anyway. At the level of original art, pastiche is really only useful as an aid to musical literacy, to help a composer to acquire the ability to notate his ideas quickly and precisely.

This book, from Chapter 2 onwards, stems from teaching undergraduate music students for many years. However highly qualified they may be on entry to University, present school examination options produce wide disparities between them in reading and manipulating notes on paper and in analytical skills. Fine performers often cannot read without their instruments: many excellent historians of musical information have missed out the study of the techniques, of which harmony is one, for analysing the music itself. Even those who have been through traditional 'harmony' courses often have a generous vocabulary of vertical chords but little grasp of the contexts in which they may occur or of their implicit horizontal drive. A harmony is meaningless in isolation. It takes on meaning only in a time continuum. Its sense of motion, where it has come from and where it is probably going, is a powerful force, whether presented chord-by-chord as in a hymn or in the lines of counterpoint in a fugue or a canon.

The first chapter has been added to make the material accessible to anyone with a sound grasp of rudiments. A knowledge is assumed of notational conventions, key signatures, major and minor scales and intervals. Given this minimum foundation, the book can be used in various ways.

As a text-book for students at school or college it provides a coherent plan for starting harmony from scratch. In this case, teachers will want to slow down the pace at which ideas are presented, and to develop in their own words points as they arise. They will need to select exercises, and add to the number and range of 'supplementary' exercises, in response to the individual needs of their students. The supplementary exercises are offered only as suggestions. More can be invented indefinitely, developing over a longer musical time-span and reaching chronologically forward and back through the whole repertoire of tonal music.

For those who have already studied harmony to some level, the book can be used to cast new light on harmonic processes. In this case the pace will be different: the first two chapters may appear more or less self-evident and only need reading through quickly with selected exercises worked to confirm the student's grasp of the principles involved. Later chapters will need a much more thorough approach: there are few first-year undergraduate music students who can imitate a dozen bars of a Mozart piano sonata, let alone a whole movement, well enough to deceive the informed ear. Again, tutors will probably wish to control the pace and adjust the range of exercises to individual requirements.

For the interested amateur listener, the book provides an insight into the dynamics of harmony even if the exercises are not worked through systematically. Simply reading through the text and thoughtfully playing the examples on piano or gramophone will awaken an awareness of how at least three composers sustain a harmonic impetus in their music.

For the performer, amateur and professional alike, a grasp of compositional principles including the vertical and horizontal implications of harmony is essential. The recognition of the nature of a dissonance or the tension of an unexpected change of harmonic direction is a vital step towards deciding how it should be played. The memorising feats suggested in some of the 'mental hearing and analysis' exercises are also of immediate practical value to performers whether they choose to play wholly from memory or simply need release from being 'copy-bound' as they practise.

Because points are made succinctly and are illustrated by the music itself rather than by verbiage about music, presentation of the material may appear rather dense. So for readers using it not as a means only of knowing roughly how harmonic progressions work but also to gain fluency in actually writing them, there will always be a need to slow the pace down. A single sentence often describes an exercise which may serve as the core of a whole week's work in the area of musical literacy for a school, college or university student.

Among practical considerations, this book differs from other courses on harmony in the stress it lays on dominant relationships at various levels, in the concept of 'substitutes' and the emancipation of mode, and above all in the methodological devices it suggests for developing aural perception and applying it at once and in considerable detail to real music. However, no claim is made that the actual material in the book is particularly original. Rameau recognised the supremacy of the dominant nearly 250 years ago and Schenker has reiterated it in this century.

All examples are taken from three 'core texts'. The reasoning behind this is that illustrating any harmonic device by quoting a bar or two of music otherwise not familiar tells us virtually nothing at all about either the impact of the particular device, or the music from which the example is taken. To show that, say, an Italian sixth chord appears in a given bar of a Beethoven string quartet is meaningless unless we know the wider context: is it one of many at this point? Is it an isolated moment of particular harmonic tension? Is it perhaps the only Italian sixth that Beethoven ever wrote?

So the examples in the text are themselves as extensive as the economics of publishing allow, and you are strongly recommended to acquire copies of this limited repertoire: you may have them already; they are almost certain to be in school, college or public libraries; they can be purchased in the editions suggested which are selected for their cheapness as well as their reliability. They are:

J S Bach: 371 Harmonised Chorales..., ed. Riemenschneider, published by G Schirmer.
W A Mozart: The piano sonatas and fantasies. Urtext edition, published by Lea Pocket Scores, nos. 39 and 40.
F Schubert: Song cycle *Die schöne Müllerin,* published by Lea Pocket Scores, no. 23.

They are referred to in the text by title, bar number and beat: e.g. *Die schöne Müllerin* no. II 'Wohin?', b 10[1].

If these scores are available, all examples from them should be played or heard in their larger context, a whole chorale, a whole sonata movement or a whole song at least. The sonatas and the song-cycle are accessible through commercial recordings. However, if you do not have access to scores and discs or tape, all the examples in the text are complete and all the 'mental hearing', 'analysis' and 'imitative' exercises can be done without additional material. The 'supplementary' exercises though do assume some more music, the core texts and/or anything else you may have acquired through learning an instrument or building a library of vocal, orchestral and instrumental scores, perhaps to enhance a record collection.

Note particularly that limiting examples to a single group of works from three composers is in no way intended to imply any limitation in your repertoire. On the contrary, the absence of selected examples from elsewhere should be looked on as an invitation to search everywhere for further material. Everyone has a legal right of access to public libraries. Use it. University, polytechnic and college students normally have music collections immediately to hand in institutional libraries. Browse and borrow. Or perhaps you are learning a Haydn piano sonata, a Brahms intermezzo or a Joplin piano rag. Each is potential material for either momentary analysis of fragments or, occasionally, 'total analysis' to assess the impact of every note. Perhaps you are not a performer at all. Recordings and matching scores provide limitless material, and everyone has a voice with which to sing.

Neither 'mental hearing' nor 'analysis' need mean a formal period of time spent poring over a score at piano or desk but includes recognising by ear the opening progression of a movement heard on radio or a TV advertising theme, or a fragment of 'Muzak' in a supermarket.

'Imitation' need not mean extensive written exercises in only three styles: improvise at the keyboard an alternative eight bars of a dance movement from a baroque harpsichord suite or an additional verse of a Cole Porter song if your current interest has steeped you in one or other of these idioms; create in your head the opening of a Vivaldian concerto, or of a Slavonic dance to add to those of Dvořák.

The most precious quality you can cultivate is the kind of musical inquisitiveness and curiosity which is implied by these suggestions. Attitudes of mind and a lateral and inventive imagination contribute more to the development of a perceptive ear and accuracy in analysis and notation than any planned course of study, however conscientiously you follow it.

From a teacher's point of view, such permissiveness may present a dilemma: will such freedom lead to misunderstanding by students and to the study and absorption of their own errors? Experience strongly suggests that a few grammatical mistakes which can be identified and corrected by a tutor are far preferable to the sense of inhibition and of being hedged round by rules which leads to the composing of a style of 'music' only found in text-books.

Very little historical perspective is explained: a history of the sparking-plug will not help you to dismantle or assemble the lawn-mower. At times though such background information can clarify a point, and it is then provided.

No book on harmony can claim to be exhaustive and this one is no exception. It does not explain every possible harmonic phenomenon through the whole 350 years and more of the tonal tradition. Instead, it is concerned with what actually happens in a limited range of musical structures and idioms. Given a sound methodology, you can extend this experience for yourself, by analogy, by further reading and, above all, by listening. The fundamental processes in tonal harmony are common throughout. It is the time-span, the selection and density of dissonances and the range of tonal excursions which change with the centuries.

Untwisting all the chains that tie
The hidden soul of harmony

(Milton: L'Allegro)

CHAPTER 1

Static Harmony, Consonance and Dissonance

1.1 TRIADS

Harmony consists of vertically constructed chords and their horizontal relationship to each other. The smallest number of notes which will create self-sufficient and consonant harmony as opposed to a single note, is two, the ROOT and the THIRD. The density of this sound is increased by the addition of a FIFTH to create a TRIAD, three notes such as those in Ex. 1a. Whether the third is major or minor determines the 'major' or 'minor' character of the chord. Triads with major thirds are conventionally indicated by capital Roman numerals, 'I', 'V', etc. Lower case numerals, 'i', 'ii', 'vi', indicate triads with minor thirds.

Ex. 1a Triads in C major

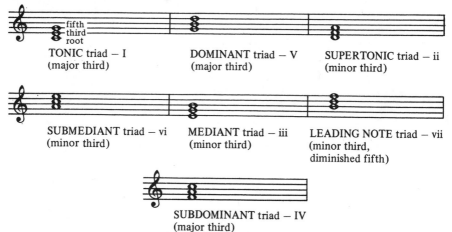

Such ROOT POSITION chords can be described by the figures $\frac{5}{3}$ implying the presence above a bass note of a third and a fifth.

1.2 *Mental hearing and analysis exercise*
Sit at a keyboard instrument and shape your hand so that you are bound to play a triad. Shut your eyes and play triads at random. Identify them

aurally as major or minor (defined by the third) or diminished (defined by a minor third and a diminished fifth). Use your eyes to help only if you are uncertain after hearing them.

3 A purely theoretical approach to minor keys, 'melodic' and 'harmonic', introduces a host of unnecessary complications: raised or lowered submediants and leading notes seems to create augmented and diminished triads of bewildering variety.

In fact:

(a) Where a composer sticks rigidly to a minor key, only some of the apparent options occur regularly.

Ex. 1b shows the triads most usually encountered in music constrained by 'c minor'.

Play these triads. You will find that ii and vii sound cramped because of their diminished fifth. This quality is relieved by inversion, to be discussed later.

(b) As Chapter 3 will explain, 'minor' and 'major' are not as distinct from each other as distilled theorising may suggest. Some minor-key chords altered by accidentals are no more than welcome visitors from the major side.

Ex. 1b

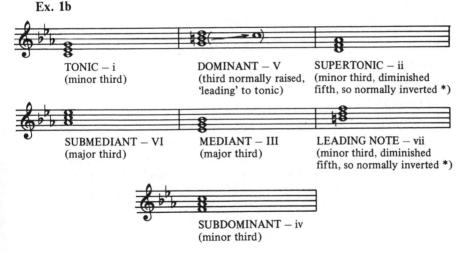

TONIC – i
(minor third)

DOMINANT – V
(third normally raised, 'leading' to tonic)

SUPERTONIC – ii
(minor third, diminished fifth, so normally inverted *)

SUBMEDIANT – VI
(major third)

MEDIANT – III
(major third)

LEADING NOTE – vii
(minor third, diminished fifth, so normally inverted *)

SUBDOMINANT – iv
(minor third)

1.4 CONSONANCE AND DISSONANCE

These are easier to hear than to explain in words.

1.4.1 A valuable aural exercise, to repeat for as many weeks or months as are needed to achieve absolute accuracy, is to play two notes on the piano, one

---

*Inversions are explained in 1.5.

It is not too soon to suggest that, in some contexts, vii does not really exist at all but is a version of V (10.6.1. examines this notion further). In other cases the predictability of harmony following well-tried patterns can make even the most obtuse sounds including diminished triads acceptable for a moment: this too is discussed later (7.4).

with each hand, at random and with your eyes closed. Name the interval they make and then confirm your accuracy by looking at the keyboard. At first, keep within one octave.

1.4.2 Alternatively select an interval by nomenclature, 'perfect fifth', 'minor third', and then sing, hum or imagine its two component notes, beginning with the lower one.

1.4.3 You will probably conclude something along the following lines:

(a) consonant and potentially final sounds are unison, octave and major or minor thirds.

(b) Also consonant are perfect fifths (too empty, though, to be satisfactorily sustained without an intervening third) and perfect fourths (but top-heavy and anything but a feasible *final* sound. Heard above a bass note, a perfect fourth is indeed considered dissonant).

(c) Consonant, but not potentially final, are sixths, major and minor.

(d) The remainder, major and minor seconds, augmented fourth/diminished fifth and major and minor sevenths, are dissonant to a greater or lesser extent.

1.4.4 Do not associate 'consonant' with 'desirable' or 'good' and 'dissonant' with 'bad' or 'ugly'. Wholly consonant music would be short-lived indeed thanks to its tedium. In the context of tonal harmony, unrelieved dissonance too would pall: and the very sense of dissonance itself would be lost without relative consonance with which to create, in turn, tension and release.

1.5 INVERSIONS

Triads can be put into 'first inversion' by taking the root from the bottom, leaving the third functioning as a bass note. The notes above the bass then will be $^6_3$, 6 denoting the root and 3 the fifth. (The names 'root' and 'fifth' etc. are retained although they are not now at this distance from the bass). The distribution of notes above the bass notes does not affect the way the chord is described: both chords marked * in Ex. 1c are first inversions of ii, the supertonic, in C major. Another musical short-hand is, for root position, 'a', and for first inversion, 'b'.

Ex. 1c Inverting I and ii in C major

Ia	Ib	iia	iib	iia	iib
$\binom{5}{3}$	$\binom{6}{3}$	$\binom{5}{3}$	$\binom{6}{3}$	$\binom{5}{3}$	$\binom{6}{3}$

Inversion relieves diminished triads such as vii, or ii in the minor mode, of their cramped quality. While seldom found in root position, in first inversion they are thoroughly acceptable. Play Ex. 1d.

Ex. 1d iia and iib in the minor mode

iia   iib

6   Triads are NOT used indiscriminately in *second* inversion, i.e. with the third also taken from the bottom, leaving the *fifth* functioning as a bass note. Avoid this (denoted as e.g. Ic, iic, etc.) at all costs until you have read Chapter 6.

7   SEVENTHS

Chords often have a further note, a seventh, added to the heap of thirds which make a triad. Details of their treatment are found first in Chapter 2, but it is as well to be aware of their presence already. They are denoted V^7, ii^7, etc.

The addition of a seventh enriches a chord sufficiently for it to sound complete, though anything but stable or final, in second inversion. By counting up from the bass note you can calculate the figuring: $\frac{6}{4}$, e.g.

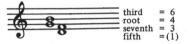

third	=	6
root	=	4
seventh	=	3
fifth	=	(1)

or, in C major, V^7c; 'V' = dominant, '7' = with a seventh added, 'c' = with not root, nor third, but fifth as the bass note.

To complete a picture which we shall not look at again until later, work out the figuring for the *last* inversion of the dominant seventh. Then, having done so, look below.

Specimen answer:

fifth	=	6	
third	=	4	– i.e. V^7d.
root	=	2	
seventh	=	(1)	

.8   Ninths are also added though much less frequently, and then often with the ninth as a decoration such as an appoggiatura.*

.9   Exs. 1e, 1f and 1g show some root position and first inversion harmony with an additional bass line showing the roots of all the chords.

---

*By the beginning of the twentieth century, ninths, elevenths and thirteenths create self-standing chords of up to seven different notes, but these do not belong to the styles of the three 'core texts', Bach chorale harmonizations, Mozart piano sonatas and Schubert's song-cycle *Die schöne Müllerin*.

Ex. 1e   Bach: R(iemenschneider) 80, chorale harmonisation, 'O Haupt voll Blut und Wunden', bb1–2

Fundamental bass

I   IV   I   IV V   I   ii   V   I

Ex. 1f   Mozart: Sonata K576, third movement, bb1–4

Fundamental bass

I   ii   V   I

Ex. 1g   Schubert: 'Pause', *Die schöne Müllerin* no. XII, bb20–3

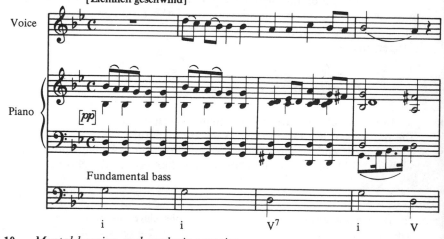

Fundamental bass

i   i   V⁷   i   V

1.10   *Mental hearing and analysis exercise*
      Take any two pieces of tonal music, the first preferably from one of the

three 'core texts' and the second as far-reaching as you like. Play, read or hear them on record or tape and identify chords in root position and first inversion, ignoring the rest, i.e. those in other inversions or complicated by suspensions, appoggiaturas or any other intensification which clouds the issue.

1.11 *Imitative exercise*
Write some root position chords in various styles: half-a-dozen four-part chords which could have come from a chorale (on two staves); some piano chords composed out into a whole bar or more of broken chords; a dominant seventh for string quartet or a tonic minor chord for wind octet. Then do the same with some first inversions.

1.12 MODULATION

'Modulation' implies the moving of a key-centre, a tonic, from one level to another. A sonata movement in B♭ major such as K333 (turn to Chapter 15, Ex. 15i) begins in B♭ major (b1. . .) but, by the second subject, it is clearly centred in F major (b23). It has modulated to the dominant.

The first sign of the moving of the key-centre is at b12 where E is naturalised. If it were flattened again within a bar or two, its effect would have been brief and less significant. But from this point onwards, every E is naturalised. Bar 23, then, begins not simply with the *chord* of F but in the *key* of F.*

Play this exposition or, better still, the whole movement if you have it, on the piano or on record or tape. Consider how far b23 sounds like a new centre. Is it wholly secure or do you still recollect the original B♭ enough to feel that the movement could not *end* in F?

The process of modulation can be achieved in many other ways and it is so easily confused with momentary 'colouring' of harmony by chromaticism that, rather than being explored fully here, it is best met little by little as various aspects of harmony are considered. The elements of it are gathered together in a summary in Chapter 15.

---

*This discussion is expanded in 15.10, by which point the harmonic principles involved will have become clearer.

SUMMARY OF CHAPTER 1

(1) Triads consist of root, third and fifth.
They can be constructed on:

the tonic	— I (= major triad) or i (= minor triad)
the supertonic	— ii
the mediant	— iii/III
the sub-dominant	— IV/iv
the dominant	— V (rarely v)
the sub-mediant	— vi/VI
the leading-note	— vii (rarely except in first inversion)

(2) The sound is cramped if the fifth is diminished but:

(a) the fifth may be raised by an accidental or
(b) the sound may be released by being expressed in first inversion

(3) Triads exist in various positions:

Root position, denoted by 'a' or $\frac{5}{3}$
First inversion, denoted by 'b' or $\frac{6}{3}$

(4) Second inversions of triads are a special case and are not viable alternatives to root position and first inversion, at least in the styles of the three 'core text' composers, Bach, Mozart and Schubert.
(5) With a seventh added, a chord can appear in:

root position,   denoted by '-^{7}a' or $\frac{7}{\frac{5}{3}}$

first inversion,   denoted by '-^{7}b' or $\frac{6}{\frac{5}{3}}$

second inversion, denoted by '-^{7}c' or $\frac{6}{\frac{4}{3}}$

third inversion,   denoted by '-^{7}d' or $\frac{6}{\frac{4}{2}}$

(6) 'Modulation' describes the concept of shifting the tonic, the point at which music is sensed as being in repose.

CHAPTER 2

Dominant to Tonic

2.1   V$^{(7)}$–I TO END A PHRASE

The progression from dominant chord (V) to tonic chord (I) is the most powerful in Western tonal music. In its most emphatic form, it appears at the end of phrases, with both chords in root position, with a seventh added to V. You will probably be familiar with this already, as the perfect cadence.

Paradoxically, it is logical to begin with endings. Tonal music is always being driven on in a forward direction until it reaches a cadence, a point of repose. But if you do not know where you are going, you cannot know what route to take to get you there. So a composer must conceive cadence points in advance, albeit probably subconsciously, before the preceding music, which goes to those cadences, can be fully invented.

2.2   The driving forces which impel V towards I are:

(1) the root of V leaping down a perfect fifth or up a perfect fourth.

(2) the third of V rising a semitone (hence its designation as the 'leading' note).

(3) the seventh of V, if present, falling a semitone. (This greatly increases the thrust of the progession.)

(4) other notes staying where they are or moving as little as possible.

Ex. 2a

The numbers refer to the points made in 2.2 above.

2.3   *Mental hearing and analysis exercises*

(1) Read each cadence of Ex. 2a, worrying out the sounds line by line, singing them, and mentally combining them into harmony. Then close the book and write out what your ear (and eye) remember. Play what you have written.

(2) Search in the 'core texts' or in any music you have available, for more perfect cadences. Again, analyse them and work out in your imagination the precise sounds slowly, note by note, part by part. When you feel that ear (and eye to some extent) have memorised all, or even part, of a cadence, write it out and/or play it if you have a keyboard instrument or guitar available.

Exs. 2b–2d consist of three such examples, one from each of the suggested core texts. Again, the numbers in the progressions refer back to 2.2.

Ex.2b   Bach: R165, 'O Lamm Gottes, unschuldig', final chords

Analysis:

(1) The bass part leaps firmly down a perfect fifth.
(2) The leading note does not lead upwards as your ear would expect. Instead, it falls, breaking the convention proposed in 2.2.2 above. This is very common in Bach's chorale harmonisations. He clearly preferred the warmth and density of a four-note chord at cadences rather than the thinner sound of (here) the alto E rising to double the soprano F in the last chord.
(3) The seventh appears as a quaver passing note and falls as expected.
(4) The remaining note moves as little as possible (though Bach had no choice in the matter since the melody of this chorale was written by Nicholas Decius in the 16th century).

Ex. 2c   Mozart: Sonata K280, the end of the first movement

Analysis:

(1) The bass part moves firmly from the C, stated at the beginning of the left-hand broken chord, up a perfect fourth to F.

(2) The leading note, decorated with a trill and a turn, leads up to the tonic.

(3) The seventh, sounded twice in the broken chord, falls as expected.

(4) The remaining note disappears on paper because piano music does not need every note to resolve visibly. Aurally, the G probably falls to F, moving as little as possible.

(5) The last chord is stated twice. First it accommodates all the requirements imposed by the V^7. Then it appears again with the outer Fs down an octave and with a denser texture, imparting a firm sense of finality not only to a phrase but to a whole movement.

Ex. 2d   Schubert: 'Die liebe Farbe', *Die schöne Müllerin* no. XVI, bb 22–23

Analysis:

(1) The bass leaps firmly down a perfect fifth.

(2) There is, unusually, no leading note as the V chord begins, though the seventh, E, enriches the texture enough to avoid the chord sounding particularly cold and bare. Because of the conventions governing minor key-signatures, the seventh degree of the scale needs raising with an accidental in order to become a 'leading' note, here A♯. The passing note, G, before it then also needs sharpening to avoid an unmelodic leap (an augmented second from G♮ to A♯). However, finally the A♯ rises as expected to B.

(3) The seventh falls.

(4) Of the additional notes of the V chord, the left-hand one moves as little as possible while the right-hand F♯ stays where it is.

2.4   *Supplementary mental hearing and analysis exercises*

2.4.1   Search for, sing, analyse, hear in your imagination, memorise and write out more perfect cadences. Look for them at the ends of phrases as well as at the ends of movements. Even if you are using the three core texts, look elsewhere if music is available. Beethoven's fifth symphony ends with 44 bars of V and I—though you will probably not choose to write this out. Bartok's fifth string quartet has a very clear $V^7 \rightarrow$ I at the end of the scherzo, enriched by second violin seeking out distant additional notes:

examples such as this are ideal material for discovery, analysis, and writing out from memory.

2.4.2 Find some exceptions to, and decorations or developments of, the usual conventions. Suggestions include:

(1) Bach chorale harmonisations in which the leading note *leaps* to the third of the tonic (R35, 'Gott des Himmels', at the end of the third phrase, G♯ to C♯);

(2) Bach cadences decorated by an anticipation—one note arriving on the tonic chord before the rest (R237, 'Was betrübst du dich' ends with an anticipatory G in the soprano part);

(3) Mozart cadences in which, while the bass moves from V on a weak beat to I on a strong beat (normally over a bar-line), the upper parts remain 'suspended' on notes of V for an extra beat. This makes the very characteristic 'triple suspension'*; play, on piano or recording, the first movement of K281 in B♭ and examine the cadence before each double bar.

(4) Schubert cadences in which the bass sits on a tonic pedal (i.e. holds the tonic note), while the remaining parts form conventional V–I cadences, often several times. (Analyse the last seven bars of *Die schöne Müllerin* no. XV, 'Eifersucht und Stolz'. The harmony above the repeated bass Gs reads:

| I v | I v | I | I | I v | I 𝄾 ‖ .)

2.4.3 Collect half-a-dozen or more different piano figurations with which Mozart decorates a cadence: K283 ends the bridge passage with a perfect cadence in plain octaves (b 21³–22): the last two notes of K281 are similar, with appoggiaturas: the eighth to ninth bars of K310 cover a perfect cadence in which the tonic resolution, marked *forte,* is also so insistently the beginning of a new phrase that Mozart allows parallel fifths and octaves between bass and upper notes. Both parallel fifths and parallel octaves are normally avoided, at least in music of the periods on which we are concentrating. Such progressions in parallel detract from the independence of the musical lines, though octaves to strengthen, say, a keyboard bass part are perfectly normal.

Ex. 2e Mozart: K310, bb8–9. Parallel fifths and octaves, generally avoided.

---

*Suspensions are explained more fully in Chapter 9.

Ex. 2f   Mozart: K332, end of first movement. The bass strengthened by parallel octaves, a normal device.

V   I

2.5   *Imitative exercises*

Using the three 'core text' styles as models, write some perfect cadences of your own. Begin with the last two notes of an imaginary Bach chorale harmonisation. Then write a Mozartian cadence using block chords, and another in which the V⁷ is spread over a whole bar with perhaps a broken chord in the left hand and trill in the right. A third cadence might repeat the right hand V⁷ notes on a first beat, above a left-hand bass I, delaying the resolution of the chord until the second beat of the final bar; look again at 2.4.2(3).

Finally, invent a Schubertian piano cadence. This might be indistinguishable from Mozart, or it might repeat V⁷ → I several times above a tonic pedal; look again at 2.4.2(4).

If some of these exercises pose problems, look for models in the original music of Bach, Mozart and Schubert. Revert for a while to copying, analysing and memorising. Above all, do not try to be different from your models.

This does not mean that imitative writing needs no creativity or imagination. Far from it. But your imagination will be exercised with recognising and applying the constraints of someone else's style rather than inventing your own constraints in free composition. A Schubertian cadence, successfully invented, may mean that you have a more detailed perception of at least a fragment of his style than is often acquired by the listener or performer who has never thought to consider the function of each chord, each note and each rest.

2.6   *Supplementary imitative exercises*

Write further perfect cadences for other forces such as string quartet, violin and harpsichord, recorder consort or chamber orchestra. Examine the music of any other composers of traditional Western tonal music and imitate their styles in these two-chord moments of their music.

2.7   Probable reasons for your cadences sounding unsatisfactory may be:

(1) Forgetting the potential energy in the driving forces described in 2.2. Does the leading note rise? Does the seventh of V fall?

(2) Omitting the third of one of the two chords. A seventh enriches the sound of V enough to compensate to some extent for a missing third.

Generally, though, chords need thirds if they are not to sound bare and empty.

(3) Writing more than one major third, the leading note, in a dominant chord. Since these have an almost irresistible urge to rise (see 2.2.2) they would either *both* do so, creating parallel octaves (2.7.5 below) or one would have the urge frustrated—equally unsatisfying to the ear.

(4) Doubling sevenths. These too have so strong an urge in one direction, downwards, that they are not doubled.

(5) Allowing parts to move in parallel fifths or octaves, so weakening their independence of each other.

(6) Writing at uncomfortable pitches such as chords grumbling low on the keyboard or lines so far apart that the middle of the texture is left empty.

2.8   I → V⁷ → I WITHIN A PHRASE

The energy inherent in V, particularly with a seventh added, and its strong gravitational pull towards I are not confined to perfect cadences at the ends of phrases, sections and movements. The step out from the security of I to the tension of V^7 and the reassurance of the return from tension to repose, V^7 to I, are by far the most common progressions in music written within the tonal system.

2.9   *Some analyses*

2.9.1   Look first at the astonishing simplicity of 'Das Wandern', no. I of *Die schöne Müllerin;*

Ex.2g   Schubert: 'Das Wandern', *Die schöne Müllerin* no. I

Das sehn wir auch den Rädern ab,
Den Rädern,
Die gar nicht gerne stille stehn,
Die sich mein Tag nicht müde gehn,
Die Räder.

Die Steine selbst, so schwer sie sind,
Die Steine,
Sie tanzen mit den muntern Reihn,
Und wollen gar noch schneller sein,
Die Steine.

O Wandern, Wandern, meine Lust,
O Wandern!
Herr Meister und Frau Meisterin,
Lasst mich in Frieden weiter ziehn
Und wandern.

The piano introduction consists of nothing but root position I and V⁷ in broken chord patterns above a bounding quaver bass. The same is true of the first eight bars of the voice part except that, in bb5 and 9, the broken V⁷ chord on the second beat is over a tonic pedal (as happened in the Schubert example in 2.4.2(4)).

Bar 13 sidesteps to centre on g minor but, in this new context, the first three quavers are Ib—passing notes— Ia and the last is Vb. Bar 14 remains on g with passing notes until the last quaver where again the music sidesteps, in sequence, to F. Bars 15 and 16 repeat the harmonic progressions of bars 13 and 14. But F is V of B♭, so the final four bars are again V⁷ → I (×4) on B♭.

In short, the whole song uses nothing but V⁽⁷⁾ and I, on three tonal centres, B♭, g and F. The progression (I)–V⁽⁷⁾–I occurs fourteen times without the relief of any other progression at all, and there are five verses. A complete performance therefore uses 70 (I) → V⁽⁷⁾ → I progressions—and yet the song is recognised as an exhilarating introduction to one of Schubert's greatest works.

Hear a recording of the whole song or, better still, play and sing it, at first very slowly, analysing as you do so. Then perform it up to speed.

2.9.2   Another example, as astonishing in view of the rich harmonic vocabulary we might expect, is the chorale 'Ach Gott und Herr' as harmonised by Bach (R40).

Ex. 2h   Bach: R40, 'Ach Gott und Herr'

Before analysing it, there are three further concepts which need clarifying:

(1) I → V$^{(7)}$ mirrors the kind of aural thrust of V$^{(7)}$→ I. Where V$^{(7)}$ → I is a progression from tension to repose, I → V$^{(7)}$ steps out in the opposite direction but still has a strong sense of harmonic purpose. When used to end a phrase, it logically takes the name *im*perfect cadence. (As it stops, momentarily, in this context the V will not normally have an unstabilising 7th added to it).

(2) The first inversion of the leading note chord, viib, is often used as a substitute for V^7 with which it shares all its constituent notes.*

(3) As the chord of G$^{(7)}$ before C sets up a dominant thrust, so D$^{(7)}$ before G, or C$^{(7)}$before F, or E$^{(7)}$before A, do the same. They all stand for a dominant relationship to their tonics; they are all 'V$^{(7)}$'s of the following chord.

'Ach Gott und Herr', Ex. 2h, now clearly owes a remarkable amount of its harmonic impetus to the thrust of dominant relationships, accepting that viib is a 'dominant substitute' (e.g. b2^2, b3^1) and that tonics towards which dominants relate may change temporarily throughout the chorale.

Now play it, sing through each voice part, assemble the sounds mentally or, at the keyboard, physically. Finally relate the chord analysis below the music to the actual sounds you hear.

10   PROLONGING DOMINANTS

In Ex. 2g, both dominant and tonic chords were prolonged by broken chord figuration. In chorales such as Ex. 2h, there is no prolonging at all—virtually all chords are at most a crotchet long. The prolonging of a single harmony is, though a vital part of a composer's craft, and is among the techniques needed for aural, visual and imitative analysis.

A particularly fruitful area for finding examples of more extended prolongation is in the dominant preparation leading into a recapitulation in sonata form movements. One of many such among the Mozart piano sonatas is no more than a chromatic scale between dominant notes:

Ex. 2i   Mozart: K283, last movement, bb168–72

*This is dealt with in more detail in Chapter 10. For now it will be best to accept viib as a version of V^7, waiting for proof until the later chapter.

In contrast, the rondo finale of K309 builds up a vast V^7 over no less than eight bars before the first return of the Rondo theme:

Ex. 2j   Mozart: K309, Rondo, bb85–93

Notice that this begins as a simple V: the addition of the seventh is delayed until the third bar, helping to create a sense of increasing tension as the composing out of the chord goes on.

2.11   *Mental hearing and analysis exercises*

2.11.1   Examine the chorale 'Sei Lob und Ehr' (R248), Ex. 2k. Count the number of $I \to V^{(7)}$ and $V^{(7)}$ (or viib) $\to$ I progressions. As all but one chord (which?) in the first phrase is made up of these, on G and on C, memorise it and write it out. (Ignore *s and †s, which relate to further analysis of this chorale in Chapter 9.)

2.11.2   Analyse bb1–20 of *Die schöne Müllerin* no. IV 'Danksagung and den Bach', Ex. 2l. In b2, the right-hand E is a non-harmony note, an appoggiatura. In b8 miss out the middle two quavers, which introduce harmonic devices to be dealt with later. In bb11–14, $V^7 \to$ I progressions are centred on chords other than G, the key of the piece.

Notice particularly:
wherever a leading note is sounded, its next function is to rise, e.g. the left-hand F♯ in b1 clearly resolves up to the G on the strong first beat of b2; wherever a seventh appears, it too resolves as soon as a change of harmony allows, e.g. in b2, two Cs introduce a tension which is released by the fall to B in b3.

After analysing and playing the song, sit away from an instrument and read through it. Aim first to hear the voice part; sing or hum it. Then add to it the bass notes on strong beats, before identifying first the vertical harmonic quality of each beat and secondly the horizontal spreading of this as the right-hand breaks the chords into semiquaver figuration.

Ex. 2k Bach: R248, 'Sei Lob und Ehr"

Ex. 2l Schubert: 'Danksagung an den Bach', *Die schöne Müllerin* no. IV

2.12   *Supplementary mental hearing and analysis exercises*

All of the following contain enough I → V and V$^{(7)}$ → I progressions to provide suitable material for detecting these two chords and analysing how they are used, and for writing out a few progressions after memorising them. Play some of them first, on piano or recording, and then read them silently. Then try silent reading first, and check on your accuracy by playing. Use your voice freely, singing or humming, so that your ear can grasp at actual sound.

2.12.1   Bach chorale harmonisations:
Es ist das Heil (R4)
Erscheinen ist der herrliche Tag (R17)
Zeuch ein zu deinen Toren (R23)

2.12.2   Mozart piano sonatas:
K284 in D, second movement, Rondeau en Polonaise, bb1–16, in which all but four chords (which?) are either I or V$^{(7)}$, though they are, in places, lavishly decorated.
K280 in F, first movement, bb 1–26. In bb 18–22, the first broken chord of each bar *is* a dominant, but with no root and a ninth added. So b18^1 is the chord of G major: the root, G, is missing;

the third, B♮ rises because it is a leading note;
the fifth, D, probably rises to E;
the seventh, F in the bass, falls as is normal;
the additional minor ninth, A♭, falls to G.*

When identifying such temporary dominant-functioning chords, a visual aid will often be the raising of a leading note—B♮ here in b18, A in b19 (does not need altering as it does not conflict with the current key signature), G♯ in b20, F♯ in b21 and E♮ in b22.

13   *Imitative exercises*

13.1   Using your analysis of 'Danksagung an den Bach' (2.11.2 above) as a model, write eight bars of piano music based only on I and V$^{(7)}$, beginning as follows:

Ex. 2m

I   V^7♭

13.2   Add parts for alto, tenor and bass to the first four bars of the chorale 'Von Gott will ich nicht lassen', Ex 2n. The 'fundamental bass' shows suitable strongly directional V and I chords, focused on various temporary centres, a minor, G major, e minor, F major, G major, and finally a minor again. Write first a bass part, perhaps all in crotchets to begin with, by selecting the root or third of each chord—use only root position and first inversion chords. At each of the two V → I cadences ending a phrase, the chords will be in root position—Bach almost invariably ends phrases with this secure confirmation of safe arrival after the harmonic adventures during the course of the phrase.

In many cases, the inner parts will direct themselves in a coherent contrapuntal flow: all the thirds of 'V's, major ones at least, will probably rise—they function as leading notes of the following 'I'. Any sevenths added to dominants will fall to the third of the following I chord.

Chapter 9 deals more fully with the analysis and writing of strongly directional and fluent parts in Bach chorale harmonisations. For now, concentrate on achieving strong directional harmony, even if it lacks the quaver flow of Bach's original.

---

dditions beyond sevenths to chords are considered further in Chapter 11.

Ex. 2n   'Von Gott will ich nicht lassen'

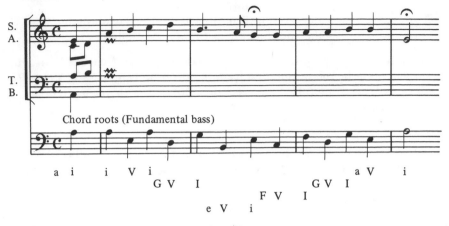

For comparison with your own working, now look at Bach's original, which is R332.

2.13.3   Look back at Exs. 2i and 2j, prolonged dominants in Mozart's piano sonatas, or any other music you have available.

(1) Memorise them (or any others you may find in whatever other music you choose), and then write them out.

(2) Write some more of your own invention.

2.14   *Supplementary imitative exercises*

2.14.1   Write out the vocal line of 'Die liebe Farbe', no. XVI of *Die schöne Müllerin,* to b13. Then, after examining Schubert's piano texture and figuration (note the repeated F♯ throughout), write your own accompaniment. Note that, in b10, the *mode* changes from b minor to B major.

2.14.2   Look at the kinds of figuration which Mozart uses to create variations on a theme (K284, last movement; K547a, last movement; K331, first movement). Then write a theme and a few variations upon it, using only I and V$^{(7)}$. Consider carefully, and analyse, the pace and rhythm of harmonies as they succeed each other: they are more likely to change over a bar line or a half-bar division than irregularly, or from a strong beat to a weak one. (If you doubt the validity of restricting yourself to two chords, hear a recording and read the score of the trio of the second minuet in the Serenade, K361. This uses only I and V^7 for 24 bars, 48 bars with its repeats.)

SUMMARY OF CHAPTER 2

(1) The progression which, in root position, makes a bass leap of a perfect fourth up or a perfect fifth down is the strongest to be found in tonal music: V → I or i.

(2) Associated with the bass leap are

   (a) a major third of V, the 'leading' note, which asks to rise to the tonic note;
   (b) often, a minor seventh of V which asks to fall to the third of I/i.

(3) Such progressions in root position are by far the most common endings to phrases, sections and movements and are called perfect cadences.

(4) Such progressions in root position and first inversion (and in other inversions provided a seventh is included in the V, dominant, chord) together with the reverse step of I/i → V$^{(7)}$, are the most frequently occurring in all tonal music.

(5) Chords are often composed out over a long time-span: the undecorated brevity of a crotchet or quaver harmony in a hymn or chorale harmonisation is the exception rather than the rule.

CHAPTER 3

Interlude I: *The Major–Minor Misapprehension*

3.1   We can easily be led to believe that major and minor are very different from each other. Books of scales and arpeggios, studied assiduously by instrumentalists and required for examinations, set out 'major' on one page, 'minor' on another. Works are described, verbally and in print, as being in given modes as well as keys. In a sense this is misleading to a student of harmony: it suggests a degree of restraint which does not exist.

On the largest scale of a whole work, changes of *mode* may be frequent and, at times, extensive. Beethoven's Fifth Symphony actually contains more music in C major than in C minor. Although the C minor opening is an essential preparation for the C major of the Finale, it might be better considered as a work 'on C' rather than as the 'symphony in C minor' which is its usual description.

In the reverse direction goes Mendelssohn's 'Italian' Symphony—its A major opening turns to A minor for the final 'Saltarello'—a symphony 'on, and around, both modes of A'?

In a sense, this is simply a semantic argument: the music remains totally unchanged by whatever words we use to describe it. Descriptions of mode, though, do tend to restrict thinking and imagination in the local, rather than general, analysis and imitative creation of music.

3.2   A single chord may be liberated from the seeming restraint of key signature by *the 'borrowing' of notes from the other mode.*

3.2.1   I (i.e. the major tonic) may become i (the minor tonic) and i become I. Because I/i is at the centre of the tonal system, a sudden change will often create surprise. It belongs frequently to particularly dramatic moments in song, or in song-like cantabile instrumental lines. So the stream is beloved $(I \rightarrow V^7)$ but also obstinately silent $(i \rightarrow V^7)$ in 'Der Neugierige', no. VI of *Die schöne Müllerin,* at bb23–26:

Ex. 3a Schubert: 'Der Neugierige', *Die schöne Müllerin* no. VI

O Bäch-lein mei-ner Lie - be   wie   bist du heut' so stumm?
(O stream let my be - lov - ed   why   art thou today so dumb?)

I   V⁷   I   i   V

Put this, and indeed all examples, into their broader context by playing and singing the whole piece if you have it available as printed music or in a recording.

Mozart develops a lyrical adagio line in the slow movement of K332 by a dramatic tonic minor in the context of B♭ major at b25:

Ex. 3b Mozart K332, slow movement

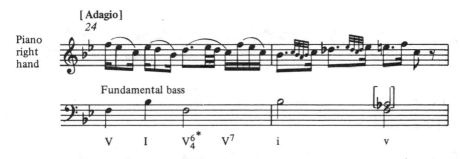

V   I   V⁶₄*   V⁷   i   v

(*V⁶₄ is discussed in Interlude II, Chapter 6).

The reverse of these two examples, i becoming I, is most commonly found in the so-called 'tierce de Picardie', the major tonic at the final cadence in a minor key. Examples are numerous (chorales, R 12, 13, 15, 17, etc.) and indeed it was a convention in later baroque music, often without the need for it to be notated.

3.2.2   V⁷ is almost always major, simply because its third also has a 'leading' function—if it were minor, it would not drive upwards towards the tonic. In some circumstances, though, V may become minor v, its third following the melodic outline of a descending minor scale, as at the end of Ex. 3b.

3.2.3   The major/minor key-signature option with ii, i.e. the choice of perfect or diminished *fifth* above the bass, is usually associated with the choice of major or minor *third*, which we shall examine in 3.3.

3.2.4   In a major tonality, the flattening of vi, the submediant chord, is quite a common inflexion. Consider the last movement of K332, from b112. If it were all in the minor, b117² would create no surprise (Ex. 3c). But, in the general context of the major mode, b117² becomes an instant of high tension thanks to the momentary borrowing of VI, the sub-mediant chord, from the minor mode (Ex. 3d).

Ex. 3c   K332, last movement, with apologies to Mozart.

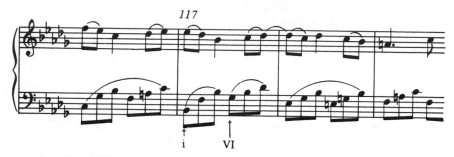

Ex. 3d.   K332, last movement, as Mozart wrote it.

.2.5   iii/III, the mediant chord, appears rarely. There is aurally no reason why, in C major, the chord on the *minor* mediant, E♭, should not appear, but no example presents itself in the core texts.

.2.6   The same is true of vii. Except for fleeting appearances in cycles of fifths (discussed later, in Chapter 7), the chord is rare except as what is misleadingly described as 'viib'. This is so clearly a dominant substitute (see 2.9.2) that to consider it as any kind of vii attributes strengths to the chord which it does not possess. Again, as so often, this is only a semantic point, but to accept it will preserve a clear view of the relative strengths of various chords and keep V at the top of the tonal hierarchy where, aurally, it belongs.

.2.7   IV may readily borrow a minor third from the key-signature of the minor mode (an essential characteristic of jazz 'blues'). An example from the core texts is Ex. 3d, b118[1], E♭ *minor* in what is essentially B♭ *major*. Similarly, iv may adopt the major mode's third, becoming IV. Ex. 3e shows IVb (*) allowing the bass to reach the leading note F♯ without an awkward leap such as E♭ to F♯.

Ex. 3e   Bach: R237, 'Was betrübst du dich, mein Herze', second and third phrases.

g: i   iv   Vb i   V   V IVb Vb i   V   i   IIb V

3.3   A chord may also change mode by *adopting, as a chromatically altered third, a note which does not occur within either major or minor key signatures.* Examples are, in 'C' (major/minor), the notes F♯, C♯ and G♯.

3.3.1   ii[(7)] may freely change to II[(7)] (see 4.5.3 below). A chorale example is Ex. 3e (†), while Ex. 4b shows II[7]b as an approach to a cadence, a very common formula indeed. A few others are the final cadences of R321, 324, 327 and 354, which show the device intensifying the driving force of cadences in both major and minor modes, though the latter almost inevitably turn aside into major final chords, with tierces de Picardie.*

A keyboard example is K283, bb21–2. Play it within the context of the whole movement if possible, or at least play the specific bars of Ex. 3f:

---

*In minor modes, of course, if the third is to be sharpened the fifth of II also needs raising to compensate for the diminished fifth imposed by the key signature.

Ex. 3f

G - - - - - - - - - - - - - II - - V - - - - - - - - - - - - - - - - - I - - etc.
D - - - - - - - - - - V - - I - - - - - - I - - - etc.

Here the C♯, the third of II, is used as a route to the dominant (D major) second subject of the sonata movement (explained further in 5.6). However, in the recapitulation, the C♯ is immediately cancelled again: the 'major'-ing of the supertonic, II, *may* imply a key-change, but *need not* and frequently *does not*.

3.3.2   Similarly VI$^{(7)}$ is a perfectly viable alternative to vi$^{(7)}$. Ex. 3g might, in traditional analysis, be described as a 'temporary modulation to a minor'. But, after the event, it returns so quickly to the centre of the G major tonality that it is conceptually simpler to see it as a brief *chromaticism* rather than a *modulation*.

Ex. 3g   Bach: R 276, 'Lobt Gott, ihr Christen, allzugleich', bb8–9

VIb   ii V^{7}c vi

Put this in its context by playing the whole chorale if possible.

3.3.3   iii$^{(7)}$, the mediant chord arising from a major key signature, may also become III$^{(7)}$. Ex. 3h shows what again might be thought of as a modulation—A♭ to f—but it too returns so quickly after the event that it is more simply seen as a chromaticism within the context of A♭.

Ex. 3h   Mozart: K280, second movement, bb21–2

I   IIIb vi   iib   V$^6_4$ V^7 I

Play the whole movement if you have it, or hear a recording, in preparation for further discussion in 5.5.

.3.4   Harmonic progressions, therefore, may imply PROSPECTIVE possibilities, but need RETROSPECTIVE confirmation. In Ex. 3f, two possibilities are implied: *either* II may create a modulation, a change of key–centre, from which the music continues in the new, dominant, key: *or* II is simply a chromatic option, implying no modulation at all. This very ambiguity allows Mozart to use the chord in both ways; modulatory in the exposition but chromatic non-modulatory in the recapitulation.

.4   A third source for a chord culled from beyond the assigned key is that based on a root foreign to both major and minor diatonic notes, the flattened supertonic. This is discussed later, in Chapter 12.

SUMMARY OF CHAPTER 3

(1) Regardless of the apparent constraints of key signature, chord roots taken from notes belonging to the opposite mode are generally available—A♭ in C major, A♮ in c minor, etc.
(2) Chords may also alter their mode regardless of key signature—ii become II, vi become VI.
(3) Normally V will be major, to retain the 'leading' function of its third.
(4) Any chromatic alterations to chords, especially making major a chord which would normally be minor, *may* herald a prolonged change of key-centre, a modulation. The process of modulation is not decisive, though, until it has been confirmed over a convincing period of time.

CHAPTER 4

Second Level Dominants

4.1   In Chapter 2 we experienced the tension of $V^{(7)}$ which is released by its resolution to I. Similarly the supertonic generates tension which is resolved by V. The supertonic is the 'dominant of the dominant', is V of V, or a *second-level* dominant.

The apparent constraints of a key signature make the supertonic appear, at first sight, to be a minor chord in major keys and diminished in minor keys. In practice however, the chord can be almost as readily major (indicated by II) as minor (ii) while the pinched sound of the diminished form is relieved by using it in first inversion, Ex. 4a.

Ex. 4a

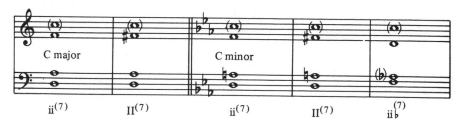

4.2   The driving forces impelling ii towards V are a little weaker than those driving V towards I. These forces, though, are influenced by two factors:

4.2.1   In the major version, II, the major third acts like a temporary leading note with a powerful urge to rise a semitone, as do all leading notes.

4.2.2   The addition of a seventh also greatly increases the thrust. In its most compelling form, II^7, the driving forces are effectively as powerful as those of V^7.

4.3   *Mental hearing and analysis exercises*

4.3.1   Examine these cadences (Exs. 4b, c and d) from Bach chorale harmonisations and identify where and how great the driving forces are between 'dominant of dominant' and V. The first one is analysed for you as an example.

Ex. 4b Bach: R107, 'Herzlich lieb hab' ich dich', final cadence

$$\text{I} \qquad \text{II}_b^7 \qquad \text{V}^{4\text{-}3} \qquad \text{I}$$

Specimen analysis: the 'dominant of the dominant' chord has two features which increase its natural tendency to gravitate towards V:
(1) its third, A, is made major by the ♮, so that it becomes a 'leading' note which, consequently, rises to B♭;
(2) it has a seventh, E♭, which naturally falls, (though the fall is delayed to make a *suspension*).*

Ex. 4c Bach: R243, 'Jesu, du mein liebstes Leben', final cadence

Ex. 4d Bach: R248, 'Sei Lob und Ehr', final cadence

3.2 Now write one or two of these cadential formulae down from memory.
3.3 Study the first sixteen bars of K311, Ex. 4e, and make a harmonic analysis of it. Check your conclusions against the specimen analysis below.

---

*Suspensions are discussed further in Chapter 9.

Ex. 4e Mozart: K311

D major

I	♩	I	*V⁷	I ------------------------	I ---------- ii⁷	V⁷	

I	♩	I	*V⁷	I ------------------------	I --------- ii⁷	V⁷	

I ------------------------	V⁷ -----------------------	V⁷ -----------------------	

I ------------------------	I ------------------------	ii ----------------- II	

V⁷	I	V⁷	I	V⁷	I V⁷	I	V	I	V	I	V

*This could be analysed as either passing notes, in thirds and decorated, or containing enough notes V⁷ to sound as a V between two Is.

4   *Supplementary mental hearing and analysis exercises*

4.1   Search for more cadences using ii$^{(7)}$ → V and II$^{(7)}$ → V in Bach chorale harmonisations, or indeed anywhere else. Come to a conclusion about how frequently the ii$^{(7)}$/II$^{(7)}$ appears in root position or first inversion.

4.2   Search for the (rarer) instances in which a chorale phrase *begins* with [I] → ii → V etc. One example is the opening of 'In allen meinen Taten', R140.

4.3   However, the progression I → ii → V is rather more common in Mozart. The first sixteen bars of the development section of·K332, first movement, is an example. Find some more: play them: listen to other performances on record.

4.4   Read any, or all, of the fragments you have been analysing (4.4.1–3 above) away from a keyboard. By combining silent hearing and an aural memory of whatever you may have played, memorise some progressions exactly enough to be able to write them down. Remember dynamics, phrasing and slurs, and any marks of articulation: they are all an integral part of the music.

5   Three points need to be grasped before you work the imitative exercises using second-level dominant chords.

5.1   Leading notes and sevenths have such a strong directional pull that they are almost never doubled in a chord. If they were doubled, either one of them would not move in its most natural direction, or they would move in parallel octaves, losing the independence which is desirable in traditional harmonic progressions (See 2.7.3/2.7.4). This applies to actual leading notes (the third of V which leads to the tonic) and also to *temporary* leading notes—the 'major'-ed third of II which leads to the dominant, and other major thirds of chords which stand in dominant relationships to each other (Chapter 5 explains this further).

5.2   Sevenths, in the harmony of the periods we are considering, are dissonant enough to need a *raison d'être,* or a warning that they may occur. So the ear is warned by the note appearing first in the previous chord as a *preparation,* before asserting the *sounding* of the seventh, and finally *resolving* it downwards. In Ex. 4c the seventh of ii, G in the tenor, is heralded by the G of the previous chord. By the early eighteenth century, though, sevenths of 'first-level' dominants, of V, were so common that they were often unprepared. All these chords with dominant characteristics can introduce sevenths *in passing* as in the penultimate chord of Ex. 4c.

5.3   You may still be misled into believing that an extra accidental means that a phrase is moving towards a new key centre, is modulating. But the chord of D major, with its sharpened F, in C, often means no more than that the composer has exercised an aural right to employ a *major* chord despite the constraints of the key signature. So II (major) → V is not in itself a modulation to the dominant, as 3.3.1 made clear.

6   *Imitative exercises*

6.1   Harmonise the chorale melody 'Lobt Gott, ihr Christen allzugleich' (R276), Ex. 4f below, using only ii/II, V and I, with sevenths where apt. To handle the second phrase, you need to realise that II of G is V of D.

Begin with a 'fundamental bass', i.e. root position indications of chords. This is far more important than the completion of three convincingly fluent and contrapuntal additional voices which may be better left until after Chapter 9. However, reading 2.13.2 will also be helpful.

Remember: V gravitates towards I
     ii and, particularly, II gravitate towards V
     I steps off to ii/II or to V
  But V seldom goes to ii/II
     ii/II seldom go to I

Ex. 4f 'Lobt Gott, ihr Christen, allzugleich'

(Do not be disappointed if you compare your working with Bach's. He was not restricted to three chords as you, temporarily and voluntarily, are.)

4.6.2 The first sixteen bars of the Rondeau of K284, which you may have analysed as a supplementary exercise in 2.12.2, can now be material for imitation. The second quaver of b8 and the last beat of b15 are ii chords. Assimilate its textures and figurations and then, using Mozart's harmonic scheme, write another version, in a different key. A suggested opening might be Ex. 4g.

4.7 *Supplementary imitative exercises*

4.7.1 The choral melody 'Weg, mein Herz, mit den Gedanken' (R298) lends itself to harmonisation on a fundamental bass of no more than I, ii$^{(7)}$/II$^{(7)}$and V$^{(7)}$, though the first phrase needs to *modulate:* simply consider the chord of G at the end of the third bar to be 'I' of the rest of the phrase; then revert to 'C'-centred harmony. The fourth phrase is also rather awkward with these temporary artificial limitations imposed on your harmony. Read 2.13.2

Ex. 4g

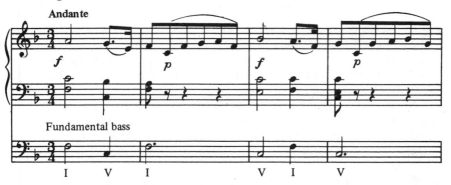

.7.2   again to remind yourself that the horizontal flow of the parts will often be virtually inevitable as 'leading' thirds rise and sevenths fall.

The opening 12 bars of the Rondo K494 by Mozart use only one crotchet chord (end of b10) which is not I, ii/II or V, considerably decorated with sevenths, appogiaturas and suspensions. It makes a suitable piece upon which to model your own similar rondo.

Begin with a fundamental bass culled from analysis of the original: ₵ I --| V I| V I| V I| etc. Then devise a Mozartian melody which fits within this framework. You may find it easier if you have also analysed Mozart's phrase structure: ₵ A | BC | BC | B¹ B² | etc. would serve as a means of expressing an analysis diagramatically, where each letter denotes a melodic/rhythmic 'cell'. Notice that the second six bars almost exactly duplicate the first six.

.7.3   Many other styles which use the conventions of tonal harmony are now becoming available. There are many eight-bar phrases of Ragtime which yield no more to harmonic analysis than these first- and second-level dominants. The same is true of all but two of the first 36 bars of Chopin's Db major Valse Op. 64, No. 1. (The two-bar exception is V → I but on a different tonal centre.) The second Valse of Op.64 begins in its turn with a deeply expressive i–II⁷–V⁷–i.

So, search for fairly extended fragments, four or eight bars each, and re-compose them as far as your fallible memory will allow you to escape from literal copying, though this too is excellent training for your musical memory and for precise aural perception.

SUMMARY OF CHAPTER 4

(1) As $V^{(7)}$, the dominant, is the most likely approach to I/i, so $V^{(7)}/v^{(7)}$ of V, the dominant of the dominant, is the most likely approach to V. When this 'second-level dominant' is major, II, its third acts as a leading note, pulling upwards. When it has a seventh added, this note falls, as is the tendency of all sevenths.

(2) Notes with a strong urge to go somewhere specific (here, major thirds, and sevenths of dominants) are not normally doubled in the finely-spun four-part texture of chorales at least. More expansive textures such as keyboard and orchestra make some doublings inevitable.

(3) Sevenths other than of V need *preparing* in the previous chord prior to *sounding* and then *resolving* downwards.

CHAPTER 5

Third-level Dominants— and beyond

5.1 ## THE THIRD-LEVEL DOMINANT

The driving force of dominants reaches beyond $V^{(7)}(\to I)$ and $ii^{(7)}/II^{(7)}(\to V)$. The submediant, vi/VI, similarly has a dominant thrust towards the chord a perfect fifth below or fourth above, namely the supertonic. As V is the dominant, and ii/II is the dominant's dominant, so vi/VI is the dominant of the dominant's dominant—the *third-level dominant*.

5.1.2 Once again, the addition of a seventh increases the thrust still more.

5.1.3 Again, too, the major version of the chord has more forward drive than the minor because the third becomes a temporary leading note; it has a powerful gravitational pull towards the supertonic.

5.2 The chorale 'Wenn wir in höchsten Nöten sein' (R247) begins with a powerful and compressed series of dominant-related chords after the step off into action from I to vi (Ex. 5a):

Ex. 5a Bach: R.247, 'Wenn wir in höchsten Nöten sein'

5.3 Similarly, over a longer time-scale, Schubert begins the breathless rush of impatient triplets in 'Ungeduld', no. VII of *Die schöne Müllerin:*

37

Ex. 5b   Schubert: 'Ungeduld', *Die shöne Müllerin* no. VII

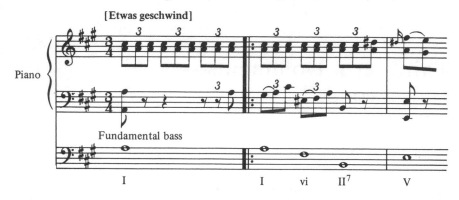

5.4   In the opening of K333, Mozart treats the third-level dominant more gently: it appears in first inversion, softening the more powerful strides of a root position bass (Ex. 5c):

Ex. 5c   Mozart: K333, first movement

5.5   FOURTH-LEVEL DOMINANTS

It will by now come as no surprise that vi/VI too may have its dominant, iii or III, the chord standing a perfect fifth below it, and in turn the rare vii is a 'dominant' to iii. Examples of dominant relationships at this distance from the real tonic are harder to find—a reminder that the dominant thrust is less forceful the further round this as yet unclosed circle of fifths we go. In powerfully directional harmony, V$^{(7)}$ → I will be very much more frequent than the more distant vi$^{(7)}$ → ii, while iii$^{(7)}$ → vi or vii$^{(7)}$ → iii may never occur from one end of a piece to the other.

Mozart, however, is prepared to destabilise the previously slow moving harmony of the adagio of K280 towards the double bar, with a step out into the distant world of the fourth-level dominant. The key is by now A♭ major (Ex. 5d):

Ex. 5d Mozart: K280, second movement, bb21–2

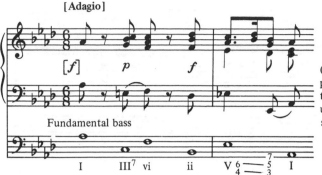

Fundamental bass

(repeated at a different pitch as if to confirm the integrity of such an unexpectedly distant step).

Play, or hear on record if you have it, the whole first section of the movement, to clarify the unsettling effect of this relatively distant excursion at the end. This is the very point at which a lesser composer might have demonstrated relief at the safe arrival at the relative major with insistent repeated 'V⁷-I's.

6 MODULATING WITH MAJOR CHORDS

We have noted several times already that a *major* chord, especially with a minor seventh, exerts the most powerful dominant drive. In fact any such chord, whatever the level at which it begins, can become a *first-level* dominant. It then serves to make a *modulation*. So Ex. 3f showed that II could serve as the dominant of a new key, in the exposition of K283. Look back at it to remind yourself. A modulating section of 'Die böse Farbe', bb22–7, (no XVII of *Die schöne Müllerin*) will serve as a more far-reaching example:

Ex. 5e Schubert: 'Die böse Farbe', *Die schöne Müllerin* no. XVII

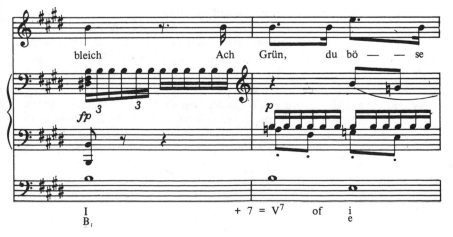

All these modulations are achieved simply by ambiguous dominants:
the tonic, B, is the first-level dominant of e (bb22–4);
e, as ii, relates dominantly to A which is the first-level dominant of D
(bb25–6);
III of D, F♯, is the first-level dominant of b (b27).

Play and sing the whole song if you have it, to discover the heightening of
tension as the key centre begins to move about. Notice, too, that this is the
moment in the song at which the miller addresses the 'hateful colour'
directly for the first time: he, covered in dusty white, would like to strip the
world of green, the favourite colour of his beloved.

5.7   Whenever a major chord can be looked on as a dominant, either in the
long term because it is V of the current key centre, or in the short term
because it is V of the following chord, it follows that its *major third* is a
leading note. Look again at Ex. 5e: here it is almost unthinkable that the D♯
in the bass of b24 should not rise to E. The D♯ is the third of B in the V⁷b → i
progression, B → e: so, for a moment, D♯ is a leading note. Two bars later
on, the same phenomenon appears a tone lower; the bass C♯ of b26 is the

leading note in a temporary V⁷b → I progression from A → D.

What then follows from this is that the D♯ of b24 and the C♯ of b26 *will not be doubled* because they are *leading notes* (see 2.7.5).
Play the following:

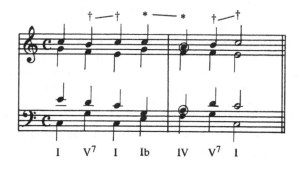

The context is C major:

> I will generally not have a doubled third, E, as it will 'lead' at times to F: I has a potential dominant relationship to IV, and realises it at *--* in the example.
> V will almost certainly not have a doubled third, B as it almost inevitably 'leads' to C, as at †—†.
> IV however may well have a doubled third, A; it would, in this timescale, be too far-fetched to anticipate the dominant step of F → B♭, with A as a leading note. The two 'A's, circled, are not aurally offensive: they do not sound like leading notes and so have no irresistible drive in one particular direction.

(All this is often expressed as a ban on doubling major thirds. In fact, the aural ban is on major thirds which are, or might reasonably be, *leading notes,* albeit momentary ones. Doubled major thirds are not in themselves at all offensive to the final arbiter, the ear.)

Mental hearing and analysis exercise

Copy out the chorale harmonisation of 'Ach wie nichtig' (R48, Ex. 5f below). As you do so, teach yourself the sound of it by reading it: first, identify the pitch of A minor with an instrument; then, working a phrase at a time, read and hum each part in turn until it is virtually memorised. Then compile, in your mind, a sense of the combined lines, concentrating particularly on the bass part (which carries the harmony above), the chorale melody, and any notes in the inner parts which play a special role in defining harmonies. For example, do not miss the rhythmic counterpoint of b3, or the exhilaration of the tierce de Picardie (the major third) at the end of b4.

At or about this stage, check the accuracy of your reading by playing the phrase you are working on. Use an instrument freely to *confirm* your reading. When giving yourself this particular kind of challenge, do *not* use an instrument until you have at least attempted to compile all or part of the sound of a phrase straight from eye to imagination.

As you copy, leave a spare stave below the short score, and write on it (1) a fundamental bass, i.e. the root notes of all the chords, and (2) a harmonic analysis, using numerals for chords and 'a', 'b' for root position, first inversion.

Note that all quavers are ornamental (passing notes, suspensions and the like*) except for b3³ where there are two distinct quaver harmonies. Apart from the need to step out from I to vi or ii before beginning a dominantly driven return to the old tonic, or journey to a new one, you will find that nearly every progression depends on dominant relationships at one level or another.

The first two bars are done for you to serve as an example:

Ex. 5f   Bach: R48, 'Ach wie nichtig'

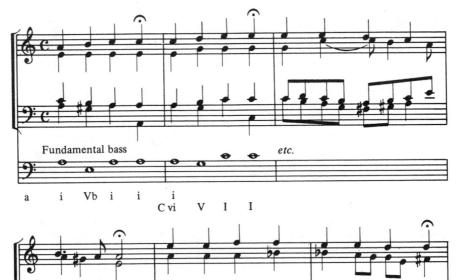

9 *Supplementary mental hearing and analysis exercises*

9.1 First, *read,* then *play* on piano or recording, and finally *analyse,* with either a written or imagined fundamental bass, the Tema of the third movement of K284. Do not agonise over dominant bass notes with foreign notes above (b4[1] or b7[3]) which you will find explained in Chapter 6, (as 'V$_4^6$' s).

9.2 Similarly, read, play and analyse 'Des Müllers Blumen', no. IX of *Die schöne Müllerin.* This is complicated by a tonic pedal at the beginning: ignore the bass A where it does not belong to the harmony above it. After V[7]c in b12, the following III[7]c is a typical Schubertian surprise which appears again in bb17–18.

10 *Imitative exercises*

10.1 Harmonise the melody of the chorale 'Alles ist an Gottes Segen', (R128, Ex. 5g). Begin with a fundamental bass, writing probable cadences first and then devising routes to them using as many dominant related chords as possible. The third phrase, in the context of D major, will allow you to reach the fourth-level dominant—try I → iii → vi → ii → V → I. Similarly, the fourth phrase will allow I → I → iii → VI → ii → V → I in G major (though Bach himself does not go quite so far along this trail of distant dominants).

Again, it does not matter if you cannot achieve the kind of flowing quaver movement of the original until Chapter 9, where it is explained more fully.

Ex. 5g 'Alles ist an Gottes Segen'

10.2 After examining and analysing Ex. 5h, the opening of the Rondo from K545, write a similar eight-bar paragraph, or sixteen bars by changing the time signature. At least, retain the outline of Mozart's choice, and pace, of harmony. A couple of possible openings are offered in case you find difficulty in getting started:

Ex. 5h Mozart: K545, Rondo

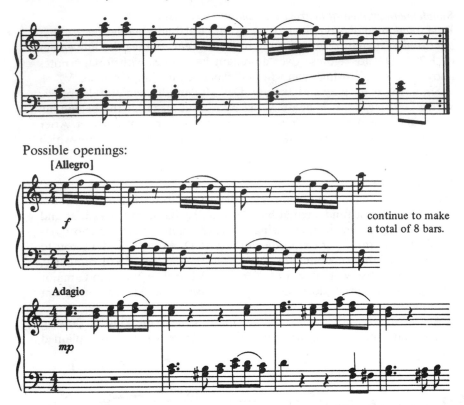

Possible openings:

[Allegro]

continue to make
a total of 8 bars.

Adagio

—this, with the harmonic pace halved, should make a 16-bar paragraph.

5.11   Note particularly that if some of these imitative exercises prove depressingly difficult, do not hesitate to revert to further *listening* to, and *analysis* of, the original. If your final piece of written music is then largely 'copying' from memory, no harm is done at all. You are not trying to be different in any marked degree from your models. The kinds of inventiveness and imagination needed are those which recognise the limitations of a style and apply them in newly-created music. It is far more valuable to focus eyes, ears and intellect on accurate harmony than to cloud your musical judgment with concentration over a long time on ungrammatical and undirectional writing of your own.

5.12   *Supplementary imitative exercises*

5.12.1 The chorale 'Es ist gewisslich' (R260) could be squeezed into a mould including the fourth-level dominant, III. Bear in mind that this is a route between the chords of B♭ and g minor in this chorale.

5.12.2   In K570, the first movement, bb23–35, Mozart escapes from the 'wrong' key, E♭, through a version of its III, G (b28) back to B♭, (b31), on to F (b33) and beyond, to C (b35). Write out the right-hand part and invent your own left-hand harmonisation. B28 will be a simple G major[7], not the diminished seventh of which an explanation appears later, in Chapter 11.

5.12.3 For the final verse of 'Wohin', no. II of *Die schöne Müllerin,* Schubert uses the same cycle of chords. Write out the voice part, beginning with the secure G major of b61. In b62, treat C♯ and A♯ as non-harmony notes—the accompanying chord is B major. Treat the B and G♯ of b64 similarly—the harmony here is A major. Two more bars return the excursion to G, whence it began. Invent your own accompaniment to the voice part.

SUMMARY OF CHAPTER 5

(1) As $V^{(7)}$ leads most probably to I/i
and $ii^{(7)}/II^{(7)}$ leads most probably to V,
so $vi^{(7)}/VI^{(7)}$ leads most probably to ii/II
and $iii^{(7)}/III^{(7)}$ leads most probably to vi/VI.

Each is the 'dominant' of the next, at increasingly deep levels.

(2) Note, too, therefore, that:

V is very *un*likely to lead to ii/II
ii/II is very *un*likely to lead to vi/VI
vi/VI is very *un*likely to lead to iii/III.

(3) Any of these dominants, when *major* chords, can arbitrarily be viewed as a *first*-level dominant and create a modulation.

(4) All major chords acting 'dominant'-ly obey the aural conventions of rising 'leading' thirds and falling sevenths, and these will seldom be doubled in lighter textures such as chorale harmonisations.

CHAPTER 6

Interlude II: *A Note on Inversions*

6.1   Chapter 1 included an explanation of root position and first inversion of a chord, if only to provide resources with which to write some harmony of your own. At several points in analyses, though, you have come across further inversions of chords which you have probably not yet used imitatively.

6.2   Chords can be inverted freely *provided that they do not contain a perfect fourth above the bass.*

6.2.1   Root position bass notes carry a third and a fifth. (The figured bass conventions of the seventeenth and eighteenth centuries indicated these with the figures $\frac{5}{3}$).

6.2.2   First inversions have a third and a sixth ($\frac{6}{3}$ chords) and are satisfactory.

6.2.3   Chords with sevenths added, normally to strengthen their dominant drive to the next chord, can reach third inversion, in which case above the bass are second, *augmented* fourth and sixth ($\frac{6}{2}$ chords). These too sound well. (Thanks to the conventions of notation, we apply the word 'fourth' to both the interval C–F and also C–F♯. In terms of sheer sound, however, they bear no relation to each other whatsoever. The bleak and empty perfect fourth is the interval which is avoided. The augmented fourth has entirely different characteristics.)

6.2.4   But second inversions of major and minor chords have a perfect fourth above the bass note ($\frac{6}{4}$ chords) and are *not* satisfactory within the context of the composer of our three 'core texts'.

6.3   There are four exceptions:

6.3.1   *The 'cadential $\frac{6}{4}$'*
This is very common indeed, even a cliché with Mozart and his contemporaries. Think of it always as a temporary displacement of a secure $V^{(7)}$; not so much a chord as a transient harmonic situation! The foreign notes can be looked on as *appoggiaturas* or *suspensions,* or a mixture of the two. So K309, the slow movement, at b5, has the V delayed by the passionate dissonance of two appoggiaturas, marked * (Ex. 6a):

46

Ex. 6a   Mozart: K309, second movement, bb4–5

What the chord is certainly *not,* is a second inversion of the tonic, despite being constructed from the notes of the tonic chord. Play it, in context, but with an F in the bass. Immediately the F major chord of b4 stands still. Mozart's bass line, on the contrary, strides on to a dominant, a C, even though it is unstable for a moment—and significantly marked 'fp'.

Play right through the movement on piano or gramophone, if you have it available. It has fifteen cadential $\frac{6}{4}$s, many the result of the variation technique with which Mozart expands the limited material of the movement: once he has written a V$^6_4$ in b5, he is bound to write another in b13.

B39 (Ex. 6b) shows the 'V-ness' of the $\frac{6}{4}$ chord by its place in a harmonic context: the previous quaver is iib, full of impulse towards V, of course, but almost never found stumbling back towards I. It therefore should *not* be described as Ic. It is a chord full of 'V-ness' which only contains the *notes* of I by a kind of notational coincidence.

Ex. 6b   Mozart: K309, second movement, b39

The Rondo of K281, b4, shows a *double suspension:* the D and B♭, prepared in the previous bar, hang for a moment above the bass V before being released to function as $\frac{5}{3}$ of the chord (Ex. 6c):

Ex. 6c   Mozart: K281, Rondo, bb3–4

To complete the picture, Ex. 6d shows a V^6_4 which is a combination of *suspension* (in the alto part) and *appoggiatura* (soprano) in the chorale 'Meine Seel' erhebt den Herren', harmonised by Bach:

Ex. 6d   Bach: R358, 'Meine Seel' erhebt den Herren', bb8–9

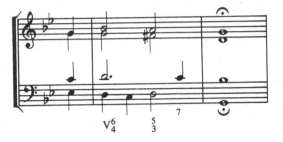

6.3.2   *The 'pedal* $^6_4$*'*
Where the cadential $^6_4$ hangs momentarily above the *dominant* bass note, the 'pedal $^6_4$' describes a sustained *tonic* note in the bass, above which parts rise to auxiliary notes and then fall again. It is therefore essentially episodic in character: it implies immediate return to the point of tonic repose from which it first arose, and it is not surprisingly missing from the dense and urgent style of Bach's chorale harmonisations. It appears, though, in the more spacious context of a long Rondo movement by Mozart:

Ex. 6e   Mozart: K309, third movement, Rondo

Discover for yourself the spaciousness of the movement by playing all of it or hearing it all from a recording.

3 *The 'passing* $^6_4$*'*
This rather emaciated sound appears rarely and is often best thought of as an intermediate stage between two positions of a chord. The second movement of K311 has one in b3, where the bass may be heard as a passing note between the $^6_3$ of C and the following $^5_3$:

Ex. 6f Mozart: K311, second movement, opening

Andante con espressione

The sonata form of this movement brings back this opening on two more occasions. Play it through to discover them.

The second inversion of a chord
with a seventh
The second bar of Ex. 6f begins with a second inversion of V^7, D major, but while it has a distinctly unstable sound, the bleakness of the perfect fourth, A–D, is warmed by the third above the bass (the C, the *function* of which is, of course, a seventh).

More subtle is b7 of R312, Ex. 6g, where the memory of the now released seventh-functioning D in the bass still warms the brief $^6_4$ which follows it.

Ex. 6g   Bach: R312, 'O Gott, du frommer Gott', b7

Play the whole chorale after first isolating this one bar.

6.4   *Above all, do not look on second inversions as viable alternatives to root positions and first inversions.* They are not: their perfect fourths above the bass put them in a category of dissonant chords which need special treatments to sound acceptable, the most common of which we have now examined.

6.5   To familiarise yourself further with the special treatment reserved for this 'transient harmonic situation' figured $^6_4$, search for further examples of at least the cadential $^6_4$, by far the most common variety. Memorise a few and write them down. Play a dozen or so that you may find, in the context of phrases or indeed of whole movements.

SUMMARY OF CHAPTER 6

(1) All inversions of chords are available, interchangeably, except the second inversion of the plain triad with no seventh.

(2) This second inversion, the 'transient $^6_4$ situation', produces a perfect fourth above the bass, and needs special treatment to sound acceptable.

    (a) it can sound above V for an unstable moment, V^6_4, resolving to V^5_3;

    (b) it can sound above I/i as an unstable pair of auxiliary notes which resolve down again to $^5_3$;

    (c) it can appear as an unstable dominant sound between two positions of the tonic as a 'passing' $^6_4$.

(3) These $^6_4$s should *not* be viewed as self-standing chords. They are *not* viable alternatives to root position, first inversion, and further inversions mollified by the addition of a seventh.

CHAPTER 7

Closing the Circle

A complete circle of perfect fifths, based in turn on all 12 notes of the chromatic scale, reduces the concept of dominant relationships to absurdity, as you will see by reading and playing Ex. 7a:

Ex. 7a

The addition of a passing minor seventh at each step increases the headlong plunge from one chord to the next: every one is both the tonic resolution of its preceding dominant seventh and, simultaneously, the dominant seventh of its succeeding tonic (Ex. 7b):

Ex. 7b

Apart from its tedious predictability, this sequence is too long for the mind to retain much idea of a key-centre, of a point from which it departs and to which it returns. Play it fast and rhythmically enough, and you may discover a sense of repose as you return to the first chord. More slowly, however, it becomes a matter of indifference where the chain is broken: it could as easily go on to infinity, or fall off the lower end of your finite keyboard, as stop on any particular chord.

7.4   In practice, of course, the circle is distorted at some point to reduce the extent of the discursion from the starting point, to control the time-span over which there may be uncertainty about retaining the sense of a tonal centre. This distortion creates a strange phenomenon, demonstrated in Ex. 7c:

Ex. 7c

Here, the roots of all the chords stand in true dominant relationships to their succeeding chords *except* for F → B, (marked *–*), which are a *diminished* fifth apart. Fortunately, the ear is quite readily deceived. After the strong V → I relationship of the first two chords, and reassured by the remaining bass leaps being perfect fifths downwards (or fourths upwards) we seem to accept the dominant *implication* of F → B. In theory, the two chords could hardly be less dominantly related: not only is the bass leap not the perfect one associated with such relationship, but even the 'leading note', the third of the chord, A, is resolved unconventionally. To reach its temporary 'tonic' goal, it has to rise a whole tone to B rather than the normal semitone of the leading note to tonic step.

7.5   You will find other apparent momentary 'leading notes' rising a whole tone too (Ex. 7c †–† for example). This though is because of the constraints of the key signature which makes them *minor* thirds of their respective chords. They can, if the composer wishes, be made into real temporary leading notes by chromatically raising them (see 7.10). The third of the chord at *– in Ex. 7c, though, cannot be raised any further. It is already major, A♮ above F.

7.6   That *context* is important in making aural sense of distorted dominant-relating fifths can be seen from Ex. 7d:

Ex. 7d

Here, a short-cut round the circle is taken in exactly the same way as in Ex. 7c, with a diminished fifth, but it occurs sooner—too soon, in fact, for the ear to recognise without a severe shock that it is intended to masquerade as a dominant progression.

Ex. 7c begins, stays and ends in C major. Such diatonic circles of dominant-relating fifths are common. An example from Mozart is Ex. 7e, an expansion into arpeggiated figuration of Ex. 7c, with odd-numbered chords of the circle used in first inversion. The first inversion of the third chord, incidentally, softens the aural shock of a 'wrong' leap in the bass—F to the diminished chord on B in root position would draw attention to the hiccough in the circle.

Ex. 7e Mozart: K545, first movement bb63–6

[**Allegro**]

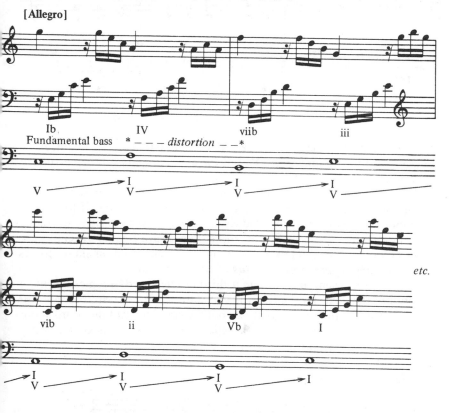

Play or hear on record the whole movement if possible, to put this cascade of arpeggios into a broader context.

Diatonic circles of dominant-related fifths in *minor* keys have the distorted pair of chords later. In Ex. 7f, Mozart remains in c minor throughout this particular section of the second subject.

Ex. 7f   Mozart: K332, first movement, bb60–5

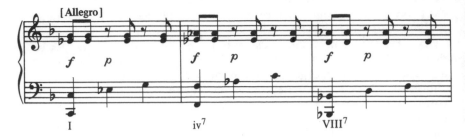

Here the distortion occurs between steps 5 and 6 (*-----*). Again, A♭ is patently *not* the dominant of D♮, but the ear is prepared to be persuaded otherwise.

7.9   This example, 7f, also shows how adding sevenths strengthens the 'dominant' drive of each chord. Ex. 7g is a reduction of Ex. 7f to its bare harmonic essentials. (It is clarified visually by using the key signature of the current tonality, c minor). The sevenths (ringed) are created by temporary 'leading notes', some major, some minor, *not* rising to momentary tonics but remaining as *prepared sevenths* of the next chord.*

You will see, then, that the *minor* third of one chord becomes the *minor* seventh of the next (marked 1); the *major* third of one chord becomes the *major* seventh of the next (marked 2): but the *major* third of the chord at one side of the distortion becomes the *minor* seventh of the next, across the falsely dominant leap (marked 3):

Ex. 7g

*See 4.5.2.

Fortunately this is all more complicated in the telling than in the hearing: the ear remains aloof from all these complexities, and faithfully records dominant relationships throughout the circle. Play Ex. 7g very slowly to analyse all the theoretical intricacies. Then play it more quickly to hear how the ear largely ignores them in practice.

10   Another, more formalised, example is Ex. 7h. Here, all the passing sevenths can be (and are) made minor, and so more thrusting, except the E (†) which has to remain a major seventh to absorb, in this part, the semitone 'lost' in the distorted dominant leap in the bass, F → B.

Ex. 7h

Returning to Ex. 7f, you should note that it does not matter to the ear whether these 'dominant sevenths' are notated correctly with major thirds and minor sevenths (b62 and the final V⁷), or partially wrongly, with *minor* third and minor seventh (b61) or major third and *major* seventh (b63). The ear always understands that each chord has a dominant relationship with its neighbours. The constraints of key signatures may weaken this relationship, but they cannot destroy it.

11   It is perfectly conceivable that a circle of dominant-related chords should display some freedom of mode. At any point in the circle a chord may be as readily major as minor regardless of the constraints of key signature. In fact, such circles as Ex. 7h are rare. The complete circle already stretches our ability to retain a sense of tonal centre, of where we started from and are probably going back to; chromatically altering many notes in a circle to make *every* third major and *every* seventh except one minor, would tax that ability very far.

12   The bass, too, can escape from the constraints of the diatonic notes. Ex. 7i delays the distortion until the sixth bass note, taking the tonality deeply in the flat side (the second bar begins with A♭ major). The other alterations therefore occur here, too. The 'leading note' resolution becomes a whole tone at †–† and the passing seventh, G, has to be major at ↑.

Ex. 7i

7.13   It may have occurred to you that the subdominant chord, IV/iv, has at last made its appearance. It is frequently used as a substitute for, a shadow of, other chords (see Chapter 10). As the first step round a dominant circle, though, it appears here in its own right: it is the 'tonic' resolution of the *'dominant'* thrust which can, perhaps unexpectedly, be pent up in the *tonic* chord. First, its root is the 'dominant-resolution' distance from I, a perfect fifth below or fourth above (Ex. 7j, 1).

Secondly, the addition of a *major* seventh to I introduces a 'voice' or part which flows naturally by step downwards. Meanwhile, a potential leading note rises (Ex. 7j, 2).

An alternative is the departure from diatonic notes effected by a *minor* seventh added to I, which makes it completely and unashamedly a self-confessed dominant chord (Ex. 7j, 3).

Ex. 7j

In this context, the subdominant was well named (by Donald Tovey) the 'anti-dominant', pulling in the opposite direction from V, operating at the other end of the dominant circle, and making I itself assume dominant characteristics.

7.14   *Mental hearing and analysis exercise*
Examine the first four bars of the f minor episode of K494 (which Mozart used as a third movement for K533) bb95–8³, ex. 7k. Begin by reading it away from an instrument, and construct the sound in your imagination by a combination of direct eye-to-ear channels and an intellectual assessment of what is going on. Your assessment of the first bar might run something as follows:

forte; clearly f minor chord (despite the late appearance of the root (2nd beat)) because of the previous F major cadence.

The bass then steps onto a potential dominant roundabout, from F to B♭ (will the next bar begin with E♭?).

The third of f, which might have risen as the (flat) leading note of B♭, actually becomes the preparation of a seventh on b♭, increasing its dominant thrust, while the fifth (C) rises to warm b♭ with a third.

As soon as you think your imagining ear has accurately absorbed the sounds here described in words, reassure yourself by either playing them or listening to the relevant few grooves of record or inches of tape.*

Now continue the same kind of justification, note-by-note, one vertical sound at a time, one horizontal progression at a time, until you have memorised the processes sufficiently to add them together into an accurate reading of the whole four bars. Finally, write out the four bars from memory, play them, and confirm that you have gone through all these steps accurately.

Ex. 7k   Mozart: K494, bb95–8

15   *Imitative exercise*
Complete this circle of dominant-related fifths. Include a 'distortion' to make a circle of eight chords in all. Begin by completing the fundamental bass so that the underlying harmony is secure.

*This continual confirming of imagined sound—a single progression, one contrapuntal line of melody, a whole phrase or more—by its actual performance is an invaluable aid to building up aural confidence and competence. Essential, too, is to translate what you read into sound by using your voice. Sing what you see, loudly and boldly.

(You can check, *after* working the exercise, by looking at the last movement of K333. Mozart begins this very circle 17 bars after the 'cadenza in tempo', though he uses V[7]d for every other chord.)

7.16   *Supplementary mental hearing and analysis exercises*

7.16.1   By playing the first phrase and then reading it, reading the second phrase and then playing it, and so on, work through the first movement of K545, looking particularly at bb37–40[3]. Then analyse the sequence of downward scales. They create a complete dominant circle but, because of the scalar figuration, leading notes do not always rise. Do sevenths fall, though? Where is the distorted fifth? Which passing sevenths are major? Why? After such cerebral analysis, play the whole movement again, to capture the emotional significance of the passage within the context of the total structure. It will not escape you that the exposition and recapitulation include a complete circle (bb18 and 63): perhaps this stimulated Mozart to use the same device to expand half a bar of development into a four-bar sequence.

7.16.2   The first movement of K570, bb109–23[1], makes interesting material for analysis. This time, worry out the sound by eye alone, slowly learning fragments and linking them together. Then use piano or gramophone to hear the fifteen bars in question and the whole movement in which they exist. Analyse the circle: it takes nine bars to make the first step, from c to f; the remaining six steps are much quicker, within seven bars. See how Mozart manipulates the three melodic elements

𝅗𝅥 𝅘𝅥 | 𝅗𝅥 𝅘𝅥 | 𝅗𝅥 𝅘𝅥 | 𝅘𝅥 𝄽 𝄾 , 𝄾 |𝅘𝅥𝅘𝅥𝅘𝅥𝅘𝅥 |𝅘𝅥𝅘𝅥𝅘𝅥𝅘𝅥𝅘𝅥𝅘𝅥 |𝅘𝅥 | 𝄾 and

|𝅘𝅥𝅘𝅥𝅘𝅥 |𝅘𝅥 𝄽 𝄾   within this harmonic framework.

7.17   *Supplementary imitative exercise*

Invent, in the style of Mozart, several pairs of bars each consisting of one dominant seventh resolving into another. Then expand each pair into a figuration suitable for piano, or violin and harpsichord, or string quartet, or what you will. Continue each of them around a complete eight-step circle, including a distortion. Here are two examples of the first steps round such circles. Complete them.

Allegro scherzoso

SUMMARY OF CHAPTER 7

(1) Dominant levels can reach all the way round a complete circle of thirteen notes or, more usually, eight.

(2) This latter circle requires a false dominant relationship at some point.

(3) Each of these 'dominants' of its succeeding chord can, as with all dominant-relating chords, be major, despite the constraints of key-signatures.

CHAPTER 8

Segments of the Circle and Excursions on the Way Round

8.1 In Chapter 7, all the circles were complete: they all contained eight chords, one for each of the seven letter names in the octave and an extra one to allow them to end where they began.

8.2 It frequently happens, though, that a composer uses only a segment of a circle to carry the musical material forward on a wave of purposeful harmony. This segment may be:

(1) a number of steps from the beginning of the circle, but leaving it incomplete: I → IV → vii? → iii?? → vi??? → ii???? → V?????;

(2) the result of breaking into the circle and then completing it: IV????? → vii???? → iii??? → vi?? → ii? → V → I;

(3) the result of cutting off both ends of the whole circle, beginning after the opening I and ending before the final I;

(4) passing straight through from the end of one circle into the beginning of another: vi?? → ii? → V → I → IV → vii? → iii??

8.3 The first step from the beginning of the circle, I → IV, is very common indeed. The chorale harmonisations 'Befiehl du deine Wege (R367) and 'Kommt her zu mir' (R370) both begin with this dominant-related step: I is V of IV. 'Befiehl du deine Wege' strides off in root position (Ex. 8a) while 'Kommt her zu mir' is much less abrupt, stepping lightly to the first inversion of IV which is even then delayed by a suspension, a delayed stepwise fall, in the alto part (Ex. 8b).

Ex. 8a Bach: R367, 'Befiehl du deine Wege'

Fundamental bass

I   IV

Ex. 8b   Bach: R370, 'Kommt her zu mir'

Further steps in this direction are much rarer, though, because they immediately reach the distant territories of vii/VII and, next, of iii/III.

8.1   These further steps will, of course, occur in a complete circle, as we found in Chapter 7 which did indeed close it.

8.2   They will also occur, by *beginning the circle but leaving it incomplete,* as a means of moving from a minor tonic to its relative major. i → iv → VII → III is another way of expressing a common *modulation* or change of key-centre. Schubert does just this in 'Der Müller und der Bach', no. XIX of *Die schöne Müllerin,* Ex. 8c.

Ex. 8c   Schubert: 'Der Müller und der Bach', bb70–74

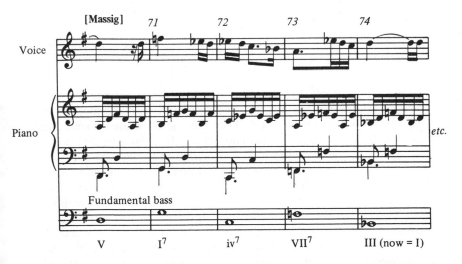

Here, despite the key-signature, the key is currently (and characteristically) g minor. B71 changes the mode to G major and, adding a seventh, makes it resolve like any 'dominant' to the chord a perfect fifth below—I → iv ---. This in turn gains a seventh and strides on to the next point in the segment—iv → VII ---. This in turn strides on, again with a seventh, to III. But III is the relative major of the original g minor; so these steps around a segment of the circle have provided Schubert with an intensely purposeful and directional means of changing key, of modulating, from minor to relative major.

Play and sing the whole song if you have it.

It may have already struck you that, by freely changing the colour from major to minor mode, Schubert greatly increases the number of related keys at his disposal. B♭ major is a long way from G major, but it is a close relative of g *minor* which, in turn, is merely a mode change away from G major. Chapter 3 suggested that the number of *chords* within a key is greatly increased if the major/minor barrier is breached. Clearly now, the number of credible related *keys* is nearly doubled, too.

8.4   An example of *breaking into the middle of the circle and then completing it,* our second category, appears in the chorale harmonisation of 'O Welt, sieh hier dein Leben', R363, Ex. 8d:

Ex. 8d   Bach: R363, 'O Welt, sieh hier dein Leben', bb3–5[1].

(V)   III⁷   vi   II   V   (V⁷   I)

8.4.1   Here Bach breaks into a circle with the rather unexpected and colourful plunge onto III. Despite the surprise, its purposefulness is enhanced by the passing seventh in the melody at *. Then the chords stride on round the circle (III, vi, II, V) up to the pause. The fact that II is major might lead you to declare that this phrase ends with a 'modulation to the dominant'. But major and minor are interchangable (Chapter 3), so try playing the example omitting the D♯ before the cadence. This would clearly alter Bach's tonal intention if the following phrases continued for any length of time to be centred on E. But they are not; and in fact the pause is immediately followed by a V⁷ → I return to the tonic chord, A major. So this is the latter part of a circle with its final V–I delayed by a pause.

8.4.2   In the light of this brief argument, it is also quite clear that the III⁷ → vi progression does not imply a modulation (to f♯ minor). Play this, too, without its E♯: its *function* is not changed, only its *colour.**

8.4.3   In a sense, we have now returned to where we were at the end of Chapter 5. There we had added more and more preparatory dominant steps before

---

*15.10   deals more fully with modulations.

the final $V^7 \rightarrow I$: first ii /II led to V; then vi /VI led to ii/II and so on. We are now considering exactly the same chain of dominant relationships, but we are forging the links in a forward direction, as music actually occurs for the *listener*, rather than backwards, the direction available to the *analyst* examining music after hearing it.

There are relatively few examples of *a partial circle lacking a beginning and an end,* our third category. This is clearly because, as the circle develops, as it gets nearer to its $V \rightarrow I$ goal, its urgency increases and it is less and less likely to remain incomplete: $V^{(7)}$ drives towards I more insistently than, say, $vi^{(7)}$ towards ii. One example, though, is the opening of Schubert's 'Ungeduld', no. VII of *Die schöne Müllerin* (Ex. 8e). This appeared in Chapter 5 as an example of the driving force of dominantly related chords, descriptive of 'Ungeduld', ('Impatience'). However, the 'Ungeduld' is perhaps even more illuminated by the fact that the segment of the circle, $vi \rightarrow II^7 \rightarrow V$, is not completed by a final step to I: E major becomes e minor in b4 and it is not until b9 that the original tonal centre of A major is finally and securely restored.

Ex. 8e Schubert: 'Ungeduld', *Die schöne Müllerin* no. VII, bb1–4.

If you have it available, play and sing the whole song, or listen several times to a recording of it. You will find that, by delaying the return to A major for so long, Schubert adds harmonic restlessness, literally the absence of rest or repose, to the hurrying triplets creating the impatient mood of this introduction.

8.6   It is similarly rare to find *a circle overshooting its normal completion:* (V⁽⁷⁾ —) I, once achieved, is unlikely to be immediately abandoned again. If only to forewarn you that it might occur, though, it is worth playing the development section of the last movement of K332 (from b91).

Ex. 8f   Mozart: K332, last movement, bb91–112

It plunges straight into c minor and then (b98) begins circling— $D^7 \to G^7$ $\to C^7 \to F^7 \to B\flat$. Whether you identify the central tonality as c minor, the opening key of this section, or F major, the key of the whole movement, this circle sweeps past to reach $B\flat$ for the next episodic melody (b112). Now examine Ex. 8g, the underlying progressions of this passage:

Ex. 8g   Mozart: K332, last movement, Allegro assai, bb91–112, schematically

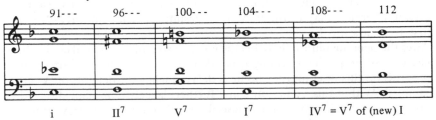

Finally, play, hear or, by now, simply read through Ex. 8e again, recognising the 'dominant' forces within it.

.7   EXCURSIONS

So far, steps around circles have been fairly evenly paced. Each chord is prepared by its dominant; then it speaks for itself; and finally it proves to be the dominant of its successor. At times, though, a composer will choose to step off the circle, enjoy an excursion, and then step back on again. Or consider the analogy of a journey, one not too purposeful but allowing time for exploration along the way. You begin with a planned route away from, and back to, home. But you can, at any point, leave this route and make an excursion, coming back to the same point or a later one, or even an earlier one, on your principal route. So *en route* through, say, I → ii → V → I, ii may be taken as a starting point for an excursion after which it reverts to its original role as a point along the main route: I → ii (=i → V → i=ii) → V → I.

In the larger scale, this analogy of a journey relates to most tonal music—all that happens between the first, tonic, chord and the last, dominant, chord of a major-key sonata exposition could be seen as one huge excursion within the simple progression, the briefest of journeys, from I to V. Similarly, development and recapitulation together represent another single step, V → I, with an extensive excursion between the two chords. The structure of baroque binary form with its two repeated sections, one to dominant, the other back to tonic, lends force to this ultimate simplification. Nor is it any accident that early sonata form too had *two* repeated sections: K333 begins with 63 bars from I to V (B♭ to F), repeated. The next 102 bars, also repeated, encompass V to I (F to B♭). (The exposition is in Chapter 15, Ex. 15i.)

8.8   The process is more easy to observe on a smaller scale. In chorale harmonisations, many phrases do actually involve modulation: the regular pace, often two bars in one breath (they are meant to be sung, of course), implies continual driving towards perfect cadences and fairly short chains of fifths: it is to Mozart that we have turned for complete diatonic circles. The wide expanses of classical sonata movements accommodate wide circles more readily than the brief phrases of chorales, and it is here, too, that we can more easily find excursions off the dominant circle and back on to it again.

However, while still begging the question 'when is a modulation?', to be examined later in Chapter 15, it is helpful to see some excursive episodes even in chorales. Play through 'Meinen Jesum lass ich nicht', R299. The first five bars are Ex. 8h.

After the opening phrase there begins just one step of a potential circle, the last one, V → I. The V, though, is taken as the basis for an excursion: progress on this brief journey home is delayed while the delights of 'V' are sampled. Within this excursion come further, largely dominant-directed, progressions; the last four chords describe another, tighter, circle, vi → ii → V → I, within the single V → I step of the principal and more expansive one.

8.9   There is a case for describing this as a 'modulation to the dominant'—and indeed we are continually playing with words: call it what we will, the music is not altered one iota. But the beginning of b3 certainly *sounds* like a dominant chord: and while the A♮s of bb3 and 4 give a more 'tonic' quality to B♭, there is no need to restore A♭ for b5 to sound like a normal V → I in E♭ again.

8.10.1   The last page of 'Trockne Blumen', no. XVIII of *Die schöne Müllerin*, takes the circle further while each excursion is very short and simple— V → I at each departure from the main route, (Ex. 8i). The fundamental bass and numerical analysis below show a principal circle of (V → I) → III → vi → II → V → I. Schubert then emphasises the perfect cadence nature of any two adjacent chords here: every pair is repeated, an insistent 'V⁷ → I, V⁷ → I', until the final V$_4^6$ → V⁷ → I. Of course, such a symmetrical harmonic pattern is reflected in the patterned structure of the piano left-hand melody and, subtly and less obviously, in the patterns of the voice part: harmony, melody, rhythm and phrase structure are inextricably interlinked. As we

Ex. 8h   Bach: R299, 'Meinen Jesum lass ich nicht', bb1–5[3]

have found throughout, from the implied directional flows of a single perfect cadence to an extended passage from a Schubert song, vertical chords and horizontal melodies and their counterpoint are indivisible.

8.10.2   As an analysis exercise, play through Ex. 8i and then compress the figuration into block chords: E $V^7 \rightarrow$ I: c $V^7 \rightarrow$ i: F $V^7 \rightarrow$ I: E $V_4^6 \rightarrow V^7 \rightarrow$ I.

Ex. 8i   Schubert: 'Trockne Blumen', *Die schöne Müllerin* no. XVIII, bb40–7

8.11   In Ex. 8j, from that most fruitful sonata movement, the finale of K332 by
Mozart, the circle is as clear as in previous examples. The first line of
numerical analysis identifies the circle: the second chord of b166 is a
version of A major (take this for granted until Chapter 12, where
augmented sixths are explained in detail). So the first layer of the analysis
reads, in the context of F, III → VI → II → V → I. Twice, however, there is
an excursion from this large segment of the circle. Before VI reaches II,
there are three dominant-tonic oscillations. The principal journey is
delayed by an excursion at the 'G minor/major' point, and stops while the
excursion takes place.

The next step, II to V, happens in two compound beats, b171^2–2^1, but
then again there is a similar excursion before the final I at b176. The lowest
level of analysis, the 'V → I's which appear in the third line, simply reminds
us that all these relationships are dominant-driven.

Ex. 8j Mozart: K332, last movement, bb166–76

Play the example several times. At some stage, play the whole movement if possible, to put this excursive circle into a context. Then omit the C♯s of b166, the F♯s of the following bars, and the B♮s of b171. The circle still works, but is far less secure, predictable and forceful. So, as the length of the music encompassed by a circle of dominant-related chords expands and as its continuity is interrupted by excursions, it needs as much impulse as it can get from each individual component chord: they are all major so that their thirds 'lead' strongly upwards: they all have sevenths added to the texture at some point. Identify them: the G of b166² is the first.

8.12   *Aural and analysis exercise*
Ex 8k includes a short segment of a circle which is repeated. Begin by reading it away from an instrument. Again, read the upper melodic part slowly and carefully until it is almost memorised—write it out from memory if you wish. Then add to it the bass notes and the harmony they are supporting. Finally, play it to check on the accuracy of your reading.

Ex. 8k Mozart: K475, Fantasia, third section, andantino

Now analyse the harmonic content. Note that, just as we have seen viib as a substitute for V^7 (see 2.9.2), so the third chord of b2 is a substitute for G major with a seventh. Chapter 10 explains this more fully.

Next, analyse the melodic and rhythmic content. They are very closely related—you will have noticed how the second bar accelerates the opening rhythm. What follows is a specimen answer to the question which these four bars pose: do not read it until you have at least tried to make your own analysis.

Harmonic analysis:

Key B♭ : I → V^7c| V^7c → Ib → VI^7c (equivalent)| ii b → VI b →iia → passing → iib | V^6_4 → V^5_3 : so the VI → ii segment is repeated.

Melodic/rhythmic analysis:

The opening pace in $\frac{3}{4}$ metre is accelerated in b2 as the melody rises in pitch, the harmony intensifies, and the dynamic becomes *f*. The climax to G arrives as it were a quaver too late, intensifying it still further as also do the staccato dashes and the upward leap to reach it.

In retrospect, the climax could hardly be greater as, immediately after, the dynamic returns to *p*, all the lines move by step, and the melody is full of appoggiaturas which, once established, lead to a more pronounced sigh on the strong beat of the final, imperfect, cadence.

Finally, write the whole passage out from memory. If you cannot do so, more or less at least, it may mean that you have not yet absorbed the points of analysis sufficiently.

8.13   *Imitative exercise:*

8.13.1 Sketch part of a circle of dominant-related chords within which there is an excursion. An example is:

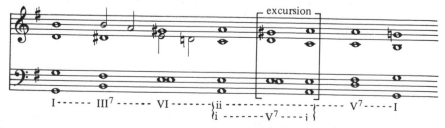

At least do the same in a different key.

8.13.2   A further step would be to use your bare harmony as a basis for a piano texture in the style of a Schubert song accompaniment. Try:

etc.—and finally look at 'Wohin?', no. II of *Die schöne Müllerin,* where Schubert uses exactly this harmonic basis for bb10–14.

.14   *Supplementary aural and analysis exercise*
The first movement of the sonata in F K533, contains some extended dominant-related progressions the pace of which is both varied and interrupted by excursions. Play the whole movement first and try to discover the passage in question simply by listening to your own performance, or a recording.

Then look in detail at the passage (it is, in fact, bb67–89) and make a harmonic analysis of it, noting too the interactions of melody and rhythm. For reasons which will become plain in Chapter 11, the underlying chords of bb82, 84 and 86 should all be considered in D major.

.15   *Supplementary imitative exercise*
Invent and write out some chord sequences which include excursions such as: I $\rightarrow$ $\left\{ \begin{array}{l} \text{vi} \quad \text{------} \\ \text{i} \rightarrow \text{ii} \rightarrow V^7 \rightarrow \text{i} \end{array} \right\}$ $\rightarrow$ ii $\rightarrow V^7 \rightarrow$ I and then develop a piano texture on one of them in the style of Mozart, Chopin, Brahms, Scott Joplin or whoever else you wish.

SUMMARY OF CHAPTER 8

(1) Successions of chords each of which bears a dominant relation to the next do not need to create complete circles.
(2) *I* (= V of IV/iv) → *IV/iv* (= V/v of VII/vii) → *VII/vii* sustains a strong harmonic drive, as does
(3) a later segment of the circle leading to a final I/i: ..VI/vi = V/v of II/ii = V/v of V = V of I/i. This is another way of viewing the material of Chapter 5.
(4) Segments which do not reach the goal of I/i or which pass it can serve to shift the tonal centre of the music, to create a modulation.
(5) Part-way round a segment or a whole circle, the dominant-to-its tonic steps can stop, allowing a harmonic excursion before starting again to complete the dominant chain.

CHAPTER 9

Interlude III: *The Linear Flow of Parts in Chorales, and Elsewhere*

9.1 The powerful driving forces in a perfect cadence led to some comments about the horizontal movement of parts at the beginning of Chapter 2, and Chapter 5 included discussion about doubling major thirds. The opening of this interlude develops these further with some guide-lines for good part-writing: note that these are not 'rules'—or if they are, composers including those we are studing in detail have all broken them frequently.

9.2 *Two parts which are resolutely independent of each other,* as the melody and bass of a chorale often are, *may proceed either in totally contrary motion,* one moving upwards, the other downwards, *or in oblique motion,* one part remaining stationary while the other approaches or departs from it. In the first two phrases of Bach's harmonisation of 'Gelobet seist du, Jesu Christ', the outer parts move in the same direction only twice, Ex. 9a:

Ex. 9a Bach: R51, 'Gelobet seist du, Jesu Christ', bb 1–4

However, parallel thirds and sixths also occur frequently as investigation of almost any chorale harmonisation will show.

9.3 *Mutually dependent parts, characteristic of classical textures, often move in long chains of thirds and sixths.* Examine, for example, the development section of Mozart's sonata K284, the first movement. Bb52–60 are made up wholly of parallel thirds and sixths with alternating repeated semiquavers, Ex. 9b:

Ex. 9b   Mozart: K284, first movement, bb52–60

4   *Do not neglect the humble octave.* Parallel octaves *never* occur in chorale harmonisations where each voice is conceived as independent of the others—the constituent lines of parallel octaves (and fifths*) reinforce each other and destroy this very independence. But long passages of octaves are an essential ingredient of piano texture, and one which differentiates this

---

*There is one situation in which Bach allows parallel fifths. It is rare but worth noting as a curiosity. An example is 'Ach wie nichtig', R48, bb3–4:

Here the melody falls early in a note of anticipation. The tenor simultaneously passes through a seventh. Both effects are attractive, and Bach clearly saw no reason to deny himself the use of both of them simultaneously simply because they create unavoidable 'forbidden' parallels. Both notes, too, are incidental to the main harmony, and the event happens on a very weak half-beat—so that the parallels do not sound in the least prominent: the ear delights in the individual dissonances rather than disapproving of the dependence of two lines moving momentarily in perfect fifths.

keyboard instrument from earlier ones, harpsichord and clavichord. So the first movement of K284 begins with three bars of simple octave melody, unaccompanied, and many lines are reinforced by being played in octaves: bb13–16 have octaves throughout in the left hand, Ex. 9c:

Ex. 9c   Mozart: K284, first movement, opening

Turn to any other piano music you have available: search for octaves and use them in your own writing.

All things being equal, parts will either stay where they are or move to the nearest available note. Fortunately, all things in this context are often *not* equal: if they were, the whole of the voice part of 'Die liebe Farbe', no. XVI of *Die schöne Müllerin,* would be on one note. F♯. (You may have learnt this song by working the supplementary exercise at 2.14.1. Otherwise, examine it now if you have it.) But where parts are neither primarily melodic and thus shaped to make melodic statements, nor bass parts which tend to leap as they outline, particularly, dominant-related harmony, they will often stay on the same note or move by step, if the context allows.

Turn back to Chapter 2, Ex. 2k, Bach's harmonisation of the chorale 'Sei Lob und Ehr' dem höchsten Gut'. Here, by far the largest proportion of melodic intervals in the alto and tenor parts are by step. The melody, too, happens to have only six leaps in it. The bass part, though, is bound to leap because it constantly describes the underlying dominant-related chords whose roots are a perfect fifth below or fourth above each other. In the third and fourth phrases Bach has filled in many of the leaps with passing notes, but your analysis of I → V and V → I progressions in 2.11.1 will have thrown the leaps into high relief.

Then, to see, in a quite different style, the same tendencies in notes which are primarily functioning as harmony rather than shapely melody or supporting bass, turn to Ex. 8h. Here there is not a single leap in the piano accompaniment, except in the bass, until b46. At this point, the sudden emergence of the piano as melodist is accentuated by the leap to the first E. (The line then continues in octaves, as suggested by 9.4).

Dissonances normally resolve by step. We are concerned here with five kinds of dissonance: passing notes, auxiliary or 'returning' notes, appoggiaturas, suspensions and sevenths.

5.1 Passing notes
These simply fill in the gap of a third in a musical line. Turn back, again, to Chapter 2, Ex. 2k. Here all notes marked * are passing notes. They are all *between* beats of the $\frac{4}{4}$ metre—they are *unaccented*—and they all fill in the interval of a third.

In two cases, marked †, the previous passing note fails to reach the harmonic security of the following chord: a further note is needed, another passing note but this time *on* the beat—*accented*.

Take care to recognise that not all quavers are passing notes. B1² and b2² both contain suspensions (to be considered at 9.6.3). B3² has two distinct quaver harmonies, I and Vb.

As a preliminary exercise in analysing and manipulating passing notes, write out a chorale, this one (R248) or any other which has densely packed quavers; omit every *passing* note but not quavers with other functions. Play it. Then write it out again, introducing as many passing notes as possible, to out-decorate Bach. Play it again. Take care that you do not create parallel perfect fifths by adding passing notes—they remain undesirable however incidentally they are created. For example, if the melody of b7 of R248 was

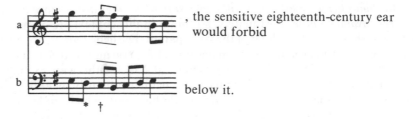

, the sensitive eighteenth-century ear would forbid

below it.

9.6.2   *Auxiliary or 'returning' notes*

These are, as their name implies, notes which have left a given point up or down, by step, and will then return to the initial pitch. The second note of each of the opening four bars of Ex. 8h, in the bass part, will serve as illustrations.

Sometimes such notes, instead of returning, escape. An example is back in chapter 2, Ex. 2h: here the last note of the melody of b3 perhaps intends, to our ears, to return. By the time it would do so, b4[1], the harmony has moved: its return to B is now no longer available, so it falls to A instead. To ascribe such willful intentions to an inanimate note may seem precious but the technical term, 'note échappée', 'escaped note', itself implies such intent—and a note is but a symbol of the will of a human composer.

9.6.3   *Appoggiaturas*

These, like accented passing notes, are dissonances *on* the beat. However, they do not 'pass' *from* another note but simply lean dissonantly on the beat before resolving, usually downwards. In Chapter 4, Ex. 4e from K311 shows several examples. In b1[3], the G has nothing to do with the D major harmony but instead leans dissonantly on it before falling to F♯ (and then slipping further to E, a returning note—it returns upward to F♯ above).

B4[1] shows a particularly poignant appoggiatura—chromatic and upward. The implications for interpretation in performance are striking—such a note demands accents of both weight and duration. It will be appreciably louder than its resolution and a little longer, too. The notation of appoggiaturas often makes them visually identifiable at a glance. Perhaps because they are harmonically illegitimate, they are often written in small, apologetic notes. Musically however, the implication is quite the contrary—they require stress to extract from them as much passion as good taste allows.

9.6.4   *Suspensions*

These are also dissonances which occur *on the beat,* like accented passing notes and appoggiaturas.

9.6.4 (a)   One suspension *delays a stepwise fall of the root.* By far the most common arrangements hold up the root in first inversion (7→ 6 suspensions) or hold up the doubled root (9 → 8 suspensions). Ex. 9d shows a '7 → 6' suspension:

Ex. 9d

vi   Vb   I
7→6

Here the alto A of the first chord, the root, falls to G in the second chord: but the fall is delayed, producing a strongly dissonant seventh for the momentary quaver. Notice two essential points:

(1) There must be a 'hook' upon which to suspend the dissonant A—it must be present in the previous chord, prepared;
(2) After the tension of the seventh, the A *falls* by step to repose on the root, G, of the first-inversion chord.

Note though that the chord is no more than a simple first inversion in which the root has become hooked up in, and suspended from, the previous chord: a quaver later and the crisis is past.

Ex. 9e shows a '9 ⟶ 8' suspension:

Ex. 9e

IV   V   I
9→8

Here again the alto A is present in the first chord and suspended into the second within which it again falls. This then is no more than a simple root position in which the (doubled) root is hooked up and suspended from the previous chord: after a quaver, this crisis, too, is over.

It is also common for suspensions to last for the duration of a chord, normally on a strong beat, and to resolve in the following one. Ex. 9f shows a '7' which would fall to '6' but, by the time it does so, the chord has changed. The *function* is as before: the numerical analysis has to change:

Ex. 9f

vi   Vb VI⁷b ii
7→7!

Ex. 9g shows exactly the same phenomenon with a '9 ⟶ x' suspension— the 9, D, is moving predictably towards 8, C, but by the time it arrives the changed harmony has made C into '5'.

Ex. 9g

V   I   iib⁷   V
9 ⟶ 5!

in a sense the verbal and numerical analysis, derived from figured bass notation, fogs the issue of the *function* of all these suspensions: all that these examples are showing is that

(1) a suspended root needs to be *prepared* with a hook on which to suspend it;

(2) it then *sounds,* on a strong beat, intensifying the dissonant bite, and finally

(3) it *resolves* downward by step, either within the one chord or to a note of another on the following weak beat.

9.6.4 (b) The delaying of the *third* of a chord produces a further rich store of suspensions. In root position, this creates the figures 4 ⟶ 3, as in Ex. 9h, while Ex. 9i shows the first inversion—the third is held up in the bass. Here a ⁶₃ chord figuring is momentarily reduced to '⁵₂' until the bass note falls to its appointed place:

Ex. 9h

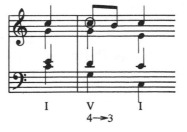

I   V   I
4 ⟶ 3

Ex. 9i

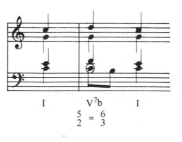

I   V⁷b   I
$$\frac{5}{2} = \frac{6}{3}$$

By now the principle of the delayed fall of the third will be clear: Exs. 9j and 9k show, simply to complete the picture, the same function in second and third inversions.

Ex. 9j

I V^{7}c I
7→6*

Ex. 9k

Ib V^{7}d Ib
5→4

The horizontal implications of suspensions in part-writing now become clear: they all begin by having a *point from which to be suspended* in the preceding harmony; they then *hang suspended* for part or all of the harmony in which they exist; finally they *fall by step*. If they last for a whole beat, it will normally be a strong one: shorter suspensions create their own 'strong—weak' pressures by dividing a single beat into a strong beginning and a weaker end.

.5 *Sevenths*

One further dissonance is so common that its vertical nature and horizontal implications need explaining. It is the seventh added to a chord.

By the eighteenth century the *dominant* seventh was so familiar that it acquired its own identity and needed, to ears of the day, no special treatment other than *after* the event: the seventh always falls.

For other chords, though, the seventh almost invariably is either arrived at by step, or is added in passing after the plain chord has identified itself, or is prepared. Exs. 9l, 9m and 9n show each of these.

---

*Do not be confused by the figuring 7 → 6 in Ex. 9j. It is purely fortuitous that this suspended third happens to require the same numerical description as the suspended root in Ex. 9c.

Ex. 9l   the secondary seventh arrived at by step

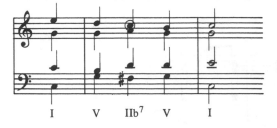

$$I \qquad V \qquad IIb^7 \qquad V \qquad I$$

Ex. 9m   the seventh added in passing

$$I \qquad iib \qquad ii+7 \qquad V \qquad I$$

Ex. 9n   the seventh prepared

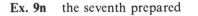

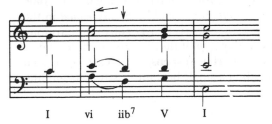

$$I \qquad vi \qquad iib^7 \qquad V \qquad I$$

Note that all these sevenths fall.

9.6.6   We have examined five kinds of dissonance: passing notes, auxiliary or 'returning' and échappée notes, appoggiaturas, suspensions and added sevenths. All but the last are horizontal decorations, ornamenting musical lines, though of course their effect is vertical too—they add piquancy to the harmony. Sevenths, though primarily added to vertical chords, have horizontal implications: they always resolve downwards and all but dominant ones need approaching either by step or by a preparatory hook upon which, like suspensions, they can hang.

Now try the following exercise in the analysis of horizontal and vertical ornament in a chorale harmonisation, 'O Mensch, bewein' dein' Sünde gross', Ex. 9o.

(1) Read it, working out the sounds phrase by phrase, line by line, melody first, then bass, then inner parts.

Ex. 9o Bach: R306, 'O Mensch, bewein' dein' Sünde gross

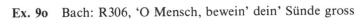

(2) Then write at least some of it out spaciously on four staves to give yourself room to annotate it, and make an 'ornamental dissonance' analysis explaining, with suitable symbols or coloured inks, the function of every note. Again, here is the first phrase as an example:

P = passing note   R = returning note   ← shows preparation

(3) Now write out as simplified a version as you can achieve, the bare bones of the harmony, missing out all the dissonances listed above. Your opening will probably read:

etc.

(4) Now, copying from your own simplification, the result of (3) above, put in as many dissonant decorations as possible. You might well out-decorate Bach, as follows:

Complete at least two more phrases.

(5) Finally, read through Bach's harmonisation again, Ex. 9n, to ensure that your final memory of the chorale is the authentic one.

.7 To complete this summary of ways in which moments of vertical harmony create horizontal implications, three more brief points need to be made. They are largely self-evident and have been mentioned earlier in passing.

.7.1 *Leading notes rise.* This applies not only to actual leading notes (major thirds of V), but also to temporary ones, major thirds of chords which stand in dominant relationship to their successors.

.7.2 *Notes which have a strong gravitational pull to resolve will not be doubled.* Given two leading notes, either both would resolve upwards in parallel octaves or one of them would have the resolving urge frustrated. This applies therefore to such other dissonances as sevenths, suspensions, appoggiaturas, accented passing notes and the 6 and 4 constituents of that 'transient harmonic situation', the $\frac{6}{4}$ chord.

.7.3 In a 4 ⟶ 3 suspension, the 4 actually *functions* as a 3—it *is* a third which simply has not yet arrived at its final destination. It follows, therefore, that *this same third will not appear in any other part while its '4' version is sounding*. The essence of such a suspension is that the ear enjoys the misplaced note: the poignancy would be totally frustrated if another part was simultaneously to 'correct' the misplaced third. Play Ex. 9f again, but make the tenor part of the second chord a B instead of a D. It immediately obscures the whole point of the delayed third in the top part. (This principle applies to all suspensions except, of course, 9 ⟶ 8 suspensions which are bound to have the eventual '8' sounding simultaneously with the '9'.)

8 CHORALE BASSES
These have a particularly profound influence upon the parts above them. This is self-evident because of the harmony they imply; but the ways in which their bare harmonic outlines are *decorated* also directly affect the fluency of the contrapuntal lines above. Their harmony is so dense that there is no time for a single part to indulge in figuration or melodic devices independently of what is happening elsewhere in the texture.

The following eight points identify ways in which Bach introduces and sustains quaver movement, softens the angularity which would arise if strongly dominant harmony were always in root position, and avoids particular harshnesses such as the diminished chords, for example vii in root position. All examples refer to Riemenschneider numbers, though you could usefully search for alternative instances of each occurrence instead of simply looking up each reference given.

8.1 The bass often changes from root position to first inversion of the same chord, and vice versa: eg. R58, b16[3-4]; R67, b7[1-2]. Note however that perfect cadences ending phrases are almost always insistently in root position. Look for some which are not. There are a few.

9.8.2   The bass often leaps an octave, in crotchets or in quavers: eg. R67, b9$^{1-2}$; R67, b2^3.

9.8.3   Unaccented passing notes both upwards and downwards are too common to need exemplifying.

9.8.4   Accented passing notes are rarer, and almost always downwards: e.g. R66, b5^4.

Accented passing notes often complete a downward scale generated by Ib → Vb and begun with an *un*accented passing note which fails to reach its harmonic goal: eg. R64, b3$^{3-4}$.

9.8.5   Where the pace of the harmony is slow enough, returning notes may occur: eg. R67, b4^1.

9.8.6   The only common bass suspension is the inverted 4 ⟶ 3, i.e. $\frac{5}{2}$ ⟶ $\frac{6}{3}$: eg. R75, b2^2.

9.8.7   Sevenths on the beat are treated as they are in upper parts; prepared (except for some dominant sevenths), sounded, and resolved downwards: eg. R183, b5^3 (V^{7}d); R186, b8^1 (ii^{7}d).

9.9   Although this interlude has been almost wholly devoted to the melodic flow of parts in chorales, the same principles apply to such contrasting textures and styles as Mozart's piano sonatas and Schubert's piano-accompanied vocal lines. The pace, the harmonic density, the strict contrapuntal identity of inner parts, may all be different, but the harmonically generated direction of notes with particular functions still applies. Analysis of a fragment of a Schubert song accompaniment will make the point:

Ex. 9p   Schubert: 'Mit dem grünen Lautenbande', *Die schöne Müllerin* no. XII, bb8–11

(1) the dominant seventh in the bass falls by step;

(2) the appoggiatura falls;

(3) so does the accented passing note above, while the 'tenor' moves in contrary motion;

(4) the leading note rises;

(5) a 9 is prepared, sounds, and falls (delayed) to what would be '8' except that the harmony has changed;

(6) a dominant seventh falls;

(7) another leading note rises;

(8) and (9): again V^7 falls and leading note rises;

(10) an échappée 'escapes' upward and then falls.

10   As an exercise, take a substantial piece of a Mozart piano sonata movement, Ex. 9q below, more thoroughly pianistic than the Schubert example above, and subject it to the same linear-directional analysis. Notes generating a particular horizontal response are marked with x: explain them to yourself.

Ex. 9q   Mozart: K282, first movement, bb1–8

Read on through the movement making a similar analysis.

Chapter 13 is an interlude devoted wholly to further investigation of piano textures.

SUMMARY OF CHAPTER 9

(1) Common and effective between two parts, (outer ones in textures of three or more parts) are

    (b) contrary or oblique motion
    (b) parallel thirds and sixths.

(2) In piano music, melodic lines and basses are often *reinforced* by octaves. Parallel octaves (and fifths) are avoided between lines which exhibit independence from each other.

(3) Dissonances resolve by step, normally the smallest—semitone rather than tone if the context provides the option:

    (a) from passing notes
    (b) from auxiliary, or returning, notes (which may, though, escape
        upwards first, as 'échappées'),
    (c) from appoggiaturas
    (d) from suspensions
    (e) from sevenths.

(4) Suspensions delay the arrival of either the root or the third of a chord.

(5) This delay requires *preparation* in the previous chord before *sounding* and *resolving* by step.

(6) The function of a third delayed by a suspended fourth is fulfilled by that fourth: it sounds *instead of,* not as well as, the third.

(7) In chorale harmonisation, basses are often at least as highly decorated as the inner parts by:

    (a) position changes and octave leaps
    (b) accented and unaccented passing notes and returning notes
    (c) suspensions and sevenths.

CHAPTER 10

Substitutes, Thirds and Steps

10.1 We have so far considered in detail progressions involving chord roots moving only ə perfect fourth up or a perfect fifth down: the powerful dominant relationship. We have met but not dwelt on chords a third apart and a single step from each other, adjacent. These new relationships can be explained with the help of the concept of 'substitutes'.

10.2 Consider first the submediant chord, vi/VI, in relation to the tonic, I/i. vi/VI shares two of its three notes with I/i, and can substitute for it in two ways:

(1) as a weaker *resolution* of the V → I/i dominant leap;
(2) as a weakening of the *statement* 'I/i'.

(In subsequent discussion, we shall assume that the minor tonic's major substitute, VI, operates in the same way as the major tonic's minor substitute, vi.)

10.3 SUBSTITUTE RESOLUTIONS AND STATEMENTS

10.3.1 *Substitute Resolutions*

The weaker *resolution* of the tension contained within $V^{(7)}$ is to vi instead of to I. At the end of a phrase, it is generally known as the 'interrupted cadence': an alternative, describing its function more vividly, might be the 'frustrated perfect cadence'. In every respect, V^7 → vi has the same function as V → I. The leading note rises; the seventh falls. It differs only in being less powerful, less final, less 'perfect'. In short, in this context vi has a great deal of 'I'-ness, not enough to be identical to I but enough to match it, like a shadow, and enough to fulfil the same function—in this case, the release in a cadence of the tensions created by $V^{(7)}$.

'Heilig, heilig', R235, contains a pair of one-bar phrases each ending with 'frustrated perfect cadences', interrupted cadences reflecting the very tension generated by the shortness of the phrases.

Play the whole chorale. Notice that every other cadence is vigorously perfect, and all but one stamp out their perfection in solid root positions. The effect then of two breathlessly short phrase-fragments being highlighted by their cadences being frustrated, interrupted, is all the more striking.

87

Ex. 10a   Bach: R235, 'Heilig, heilig', bb11⁴–13³

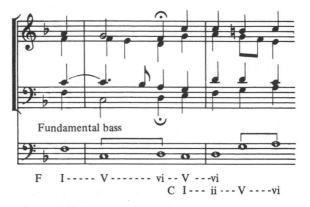

The progression from $V^7 \rightarrow vi$, already less final than $V^7 \rightarrow I$, can be held poised even more tantalisingly if the second chord is delayed by suspending it as a $^6_4 \rightarrow {}^5_3$. Within a fairly fast harmonic pace, these progressions from the Adagio of K280 must be among the most dilatory you are likely to find in the period, despite the hint of the 'dominant's dominant', II, generated by the B♮s:

Ex. 10b   Mozart: K280, Adagio, bb3–8

Play the whole movement, 'live' or from a recording, comparing the pace of these bars with that of bb37–42.

While this interrupted progression, V → vi, often appears *at the end of a phrase* as a real cadence, or at a point which could metrically be the end even if it is delayed by a device such as Ex. 10b, V → substitute I/i = vi/VI is also very common *during the course of a phrase*. It serves to extend the musical flow as a step off into an excursion: instead of V leading with some degree of finality to I/i, it arrives at the substitute for I/i, i.e. vi/VI, which in turn invites further harmonic journeying until a final $V^{(7)}$ leads to a final I/i. An example, one of very many, is from 'Mit dem grünen Lautenbande':

Ex. 10c   Schubert: 'Mit dem grünen Lautenbande', *Die schöne Müllerin* no. XIII, bb11^4–13^3

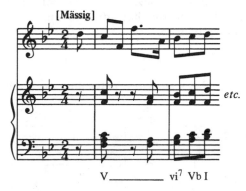

Here the finality of V → I is delayed by V → substitute I, i.e. vi. This then allows further harmonic flow, in this case a brief return to V(b) before finally achieving the goal of I itself.

10.3.2   *Substitute Statements*

The second manner in which vi substitutes for I (or VI substitutes for i—the function is still identical in either mode) is by weakening the *statement* 'I'. Turn again to Ex. 8d, the opening of 'Ungeduld'. In Chapter 8 we examined the segment of dominants beginning with vi in b2, and glossed over the first progression, from the powerful statement 'I' to its weaker substitute, 'vi'. We have actually met this in other examples, too: in Chapter 5, most third-level dominants were reached by this 'substituting' progression. Exs. 5a, 5b and 5c showed this, and your analysis of Ex. 5h should have exposed the same pattern of progressions: the first two bars contain:

I to its *substitute,* vi;
vi as (third level) *dominant* of ii;
ii as (second level) *dominant* of V;
V as *dominant* of I.

10.4   These two functions of chords, vi as a substitute *goal* in place of I and vi as a substitute *statement* of I, have introduced two new distances in chord relationships:

(1) As a substitute *goal,* V → 'vi-not-I', the progression is *upwards by step;*
(2) As a substitute *statement,* I → 'vi-not-I', the progression is *downwards by a third.*

As a preliminary exercise, find from within the Bach chorale harmonisations or any other music you have available which is impelled by the same harmonic conventions:

(1) some V → vi → V progressions in which the vi arrives as a substitute goal, but then serves as a substitute statement, V → 'substitute I' → V, the root harmony moving up and down by step;
(2) some I → vi → V progressions, where the statement 'I' is weakened with the substitute vi, the root harmony moving down by a third and then further down by step.

Examples to begin with are:

Ex. 10d   Bach: R224, 'Das walt' Gott Vater und Gott Sohn', bb7–8

I   Ib IV V   vi   V   I

Ex. 10e   Bach: R343, 'Nun lieget alles unter dir', b1–2^1

'Nun lieget alles unter dir', R. 343, b 1-2^1.

I   vi   V   I

(This progression is actually quite rare in chorale harmonisations. Once Bach steps onto vi, the urge to continue in *dominant* steps, to ii etc, is almost irresistible.)

10.5   Another very common substitute *goal* is ii replacing IV. I aims 'dominantly' towards IV (see 8.3): the progression I → ii may, then, be seen as a kind of 'interrupted progression', I → 'substitute IV'. It is, of course, very common as a starting point for the → ii → V → I cliché which drives forward so much tonal music. The opening of 'Am Feierabend' will illustrate the point:

Ex. 10f Schubert: 'Am Feierabend', *Die schöne Müllerin* no. V, bb1–3

By ascribing to inanimate chords a will of their own, (not unreasonable in fact, as they are the expression of highly animate composers with exceptional creative wills of their own), this common progression, I → ii → V → could be described as:

I, wanting to move dominantly to IV, but actually going 'interruptedly' to ii;

Then ii rather than IV is found to be the strongly dominant preparation for V

This could be represented diagrammatically as:

.6   There are three other 'statement' substitutes which regularly appear as driving forces in tonal harmony.

.6.1   The statement 'V⁷' often appears in the less dynamic form of vii. Again notes are shared between the two: in fact, all the notes of vii belong to V⁷ too. Only the root of V⁷ is missing: vii has a great deal of 'V'-ness.

vii normally appears in first inversion to soften the aural ugliness of its diminished fifth, and leads, like the V⁷ for which it substitutes, to I/i. Examples are very numerous indeed in the dense and dominantly directional dialect of Bach's chorale harmonisations. Sometimes viib occupies a whole beat in place of V in such a vigorous statement as I/i → V⁷ → I/i, Ex. 10g:

Ex. 10g Bach: R287, 'Herr, ich habe missgehandelt', bb3³–4⁴

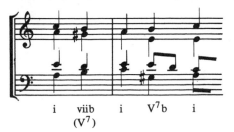

On frequent other occasions, viib fills an unassuming but harmonically powerful quaver gap between ii and I/i, Ex. 10h:

Ex. 10h   Bach: R290, 'Es ist das Heil', bb4–5^2

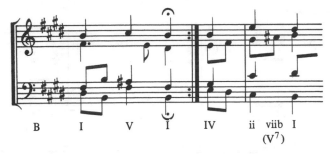

The relative mildness of viib, however, is demonstrated by the fact that it virtually never appears at cadences: after the vagaries of the harmonic excursions during phrases, the ear needs the reassurance of safe arrival at a cadence which can only be provided by secure root positions of V^7 leading to I.

10.6.2   In 10.4, ii was described as a substitute for IV because, in the dominant-directed progression I → IV, ii has a lot of 'IV'-ness (and shares two of its three notes with IV). But in a different context, IV can be thought of as a substitute for ii: in the progression IV → V, IV shares all its three notes with ii^7: now IV has a great deal of 'ii'-ness, and the progression thus retains a kind of 'dominant' quality, Ex. 10.i:

Ex. 10i   Bach: R158, 'Der Tag, der ist so freudenreich', bb1–2

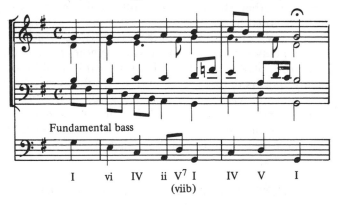

It frequently happens, too, that IV at the beginning of a beat becomes iib by the end of it, Ex. 10j:

Ex. 10j Bach: R159, 'Als der gütige Gott', bb3⁴–5¹

A less obvious example is in the Andante of K283, where a chord is built up gradually over four semiquavers, and only shows its true, ii, character at the very last moment:

Ex. 10k Mozart: K283, Andante, bb1–2

0.6.3 One remaining 'statement' substitute is iii for I. Again, all notes of iii appear in I⁷, and the 'I'-ness of iii is clear from its almost inevitably moving on to IV (unless of course it moves, dominantly, to vi). So iii → IV retains much of the dominant thrust contained in I⁽⁷⁾ → IV: in a sense, only the root of I is missing, Ex. 10l:

Ex. 10l Bach: R334, 'Für deinem Thron', bb1–2²

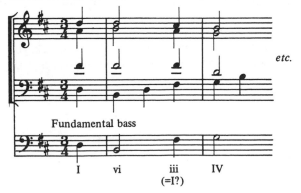

10.7   'Substitute statements' are sometimes to be found linked in lengthy chains, analogous to the links holding together lengths of dominants, but now relating chords a third apart. Turn back to Ex. 10i, which shows this clearly, in the dense harmonic style of Bach's chorale harmonisations:

(1) I gives way to its substitute, vi;
(2) in turn, vi moves to IV with which it shares all but one note;
(3) IV then gives way to ii, the strongest dominant preparation for;
(4) V (actually viib, yet another substitute).

Exactly the same progression, but now composed out over a much longer timescale, appears in Ex. 10m. Here Mozart, in D major, takes two bars for each substitution, but the vertical analysis again reads I → vi → IV → ii, and then → V^7.

Ex. 10m   Mozart: K283, third movement, Presto, bb56–65

Play right through the movement on the piano or from a recording, if you have it, to experience the sudden accleration in the pace of the harmonic journey through the exposition at this point. Compare it with the same point in the recapitulation and also with the whirl of *dominant* relationships, not substitutes, which follows at bb74–81.

10.8   *Mental hearing and analysis exercise*

10.8.1 Read, near enough to an instrument to be able to check your mental accuracy, the chorale 'Wenn mein Stündlein vorhanden ist', Ex. 10n:

Ex. 10n Bach: R322, 'Wenn mein Stüdlein vorhanden ist'

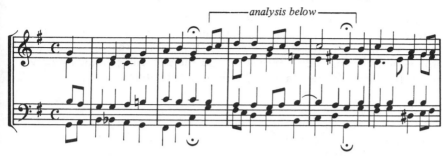

8.2 Then make a detailed harmonic analysis of it, noting particularly where chords stand in as either substitute *goals* or substitute *statements* for their more vigorous dominant-standing alternatives. An example is the second phrase (marked ⌐¬) where your analysis might read:

BEAT:	CHORD	FUNCTION:
4	I	stepping off to the dominant
1	Vb	
2	Va	aiming for the goal I but finding
3	vi-not-I	which goes to its 'dominant'
4	iii	in the bass but, with F♮ above, this actually substitutes as a statement of I⁷, aiming for the goal IV and finding
1	an ambiguous chord:	either ii with its root, A, suspended as a B, or IV⁷ which, anyway, has some dominant drive (as a substitute for ii) towards
2	V⁷,	the dominant of
3	I	

Look always for the 'x'-ness of substitutes, for the stronger chords they replace. The fourth phrase contains versions of dominant-standing chords which we meet in a later chapter. Do not expect that every single progression here or elsewhere will fit into the particular moulds we are presently examining, dominant relations and substitutes.

10.9   *Imitative exercise*

Finally, write out the same chorale melody and, relying partly on memory by now, add the three lower parts in a style as close to the original as possible. Put in, first, the cadential goals. Then complete a 'fundamental bass'. Look back at 9.8 to suggest to yourself how this bass may be decorated and made more melodic: as you vary it, the flow of the upper parts will begin to develop with the help of the first part of Chapter 9.

Remind yourself again that the aim is to end with music as near to the original as possible: such exercises as this *do* require imagination, but of the kind which identifies, in this case, Bach's originality rather than further invention of your own.

10.10   *Supplementary mental hearing and analysis exercise*

Read and analyse, in the same manner as in 10.8.2 above, the first 40 bars of K570 in B♭, the first movement, Allegro. You will find that

(1) the harmony moves very much more slowly—the first four bars are the composing out of a single tonic chord; and

(2) substitutes occur much less frequently in proportion to all progressions than they do in a chorale harmonisation. In fact, they create all the more dramatic surprise by their very rarity: bb20–23 come as a considerable tonal shock after the dominant-related predictability of the first 19 bars.

10.11   *Supplementary imitative exercise*

Using your analysis of K570 as a basis, compose a similar piece, using exactly the same harmonic structure, but varying key, time-signature, dynamics, rhythms and figuration. This will require some skill in the convincing prolonging of single harmonies: look back to 2.10 and 2.13.3. Try this as an opening if you wish:

There is, of course, no need to limit yourself to the supplementary imitative exercises offered here. You can similarly analyse and imitate any fairly simple piece or section using the kind of harmonic language we have been examining. Try 16 bars of a Chopin Valse or a verse of a Cole Porter song. See if Haydn or C.P.E. Bach pace their harmony differently from Mozart.

SUMMARY OF CHAPTER 10

(1) The dominant can resolve upwards by step 'interruptedly' to the tonic-substitute goal, vi/VI.

(2) So, too, I/i can resolve by step to ii.

(3) Other momentary dominants can similarly step to the chord a third below their expected goal.

(4) *Statements* of chords can be substituted by chords a minor or major third away. Common examples are:

vi/VI replacing I/i   ii replacing IV/iv
vii(b) replacing V   IV/iv replacing ii
iii/III replacing I/I

(5) So root distances now discussed are:

(a) Perfect fifth down/fourth up (= dominant relations)
(b) Upward steps (= substitute resolutions)
(c) Major or minor third down/sixth up (= substitute or 'interrupted' statement).

All distances are thus viable (the downward seventh, inverting the upward step, is awkward and unlikely).

BUT DOMINANT STRIDES PREVAIL, and others are substitutes for this central relationship in tonal music;

AND: there is still little likelihood of

ii → I/i: they have virtually no means of relating;
vii(b), the weaker statement, → V, the strong source;
vi, the weaker statement, → I/i, the strong source.

(6) vi/VI and iii/III have a great deal of 'I'-ness.
    viib has a great deal of 'V⁷'-ness.
    IV has a great deal of 'ii⁷'-ness.

CHAPTER 11

More Colourful Dominants: Diminished Sevenths

11.1 *The first-level dominant,* V, is so powerfully directional that it can tolerate considerable additions and alterations without losing its identity. The addition of ninth, eleventh and thirteenth to the triad (root, third and fifth) and the strongly gravitational seventh, results in a tower of seven notes, all the notes, in fact, of a diatonic scale. And still, with suitable spacings and the omission of some notes part-way up this tower, a sense of strong 'V'-ness can remain.

Such chords however belong rarely if ever to the period of harmonic history which we are considering. Major ninths above the dominant, or any other, bass are almost always suspensions or appoggiaturas. Elevenths and thirteenths have the same kinds of aural justification and do not appear as unprepared entities, chords in their own vertical right, until the very end of the nineteenth century.

The addition of the *minor ninth,* however, gives rise to a version of the dominant which is very common indeed. Ex. 11a illustrates it:

Ex. 11a Bach: R297, 'Jesu, der du meine Seele', bb15–16

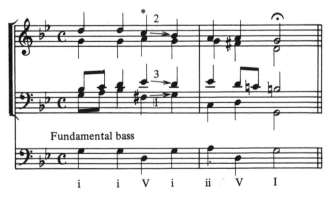

The chord in question, * in the example, consists of:

the third, F♯ (the leading note, which rises, marked '1')
the fifth, A
the seventh, C (which, as usual, falls—'2')
the minor ninths, E♭ (which also resolves down by a semitone step—'3')

Note that the root is missing: this has given rise to the name 'diminished seventh' chord, as the interval between the resulting bass note, F♯, and the highest note in the tower of additional thirds, E♭, is a diminished seventh. In figured bass, it is denoted by a crossed seven—$\overline{7}$.

The chord has several strange qualities:

(1) All its notes are equidistant from their neighbours: F♯–A, A–C, C–E♭ are all minor thirds and, extending on upward, E♭–F♯ is the same distance, spelled differently—an augmented second;

(2) The chord is therefore infinitely invertible, without altering its vertical character: notes can be taken off the bottom and put on top indefinitely without changing the sound of the chord;

(3) Alternate notes all span that most irresolute of intervals, a tritone, a diminished fifth or augmented fourth:

We shall investigate the hidden potential in these phenomena later, in Chapter 15. For now, the chord is best seen as no more than a dominant, enriched by a minor ninth, with its root missing and able to be rolled up and down through its inversions without changing its texture—each inversion remains a lowest note surmounted by minor thirds/augmented seconds: each inversion remains a chord with two dovetailed tritones.

The first movement of K332 has, in the transition from first to second subjects, two dramatic instances, Ex. 11b:

Ex. 11b   Mozart: K332, first movement, bb23–31[1]

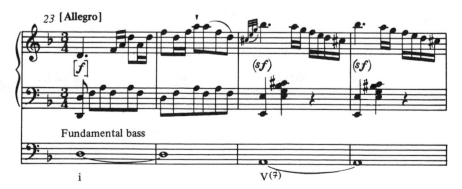

Here the chord at bb25–6 is the dominant of d minor. The root, A, is missing and a minor ninth, B♭, is added. It is hardly weakened by the inversion—the fifth, E, is the bass note—and the density of the left-hand chord, the arpeggiated stroke in the right hand, the dramatic silence below the downward scale on the last beats are all complemented by the dynamic energy of the diminished seventh chord of which three quarters of the notes have an irresistible urge to resolve purposefully and 'dominantly' as leading note (rising), and seventh and ninth (falling). Two bars later the sequence brings a similar chord, this time as the dominant of C (minor, as it happens).

11.2   *The second-level dominant,* II (major), is also often enriched by a minor ninth:

Ex. 11c   Bach: R339, 'Wer nur den lieben Gott lässt walten', bb7⁴–9

Here, on two occasions marked *, the major supertonic, II, has an added minor ninth, C, and the root, B, is missing. Again resolutions are largely normal:

major thirds (D♯) rise as temporary 'leading' notes to V;
sevenths (A) drop, once anticipating the following harmony and then leaping down but, the second time, suspended and falling as a 4–3 suspension;

minor ninths (C) fall a semitone.

Note that, because of the conventions of key signatures, in minor keys the 5th of the 'supertonic-based' diminished seventh needs raising with an accidental: F♯ in * above.

1.2.1   A more extended example is in the opening of the Allegro assai of K332, Ex. 11d. Play it now, or listen several times to a recording, and try to predict by yourself the analytical explanation which follows the example.

Ex. 11d   Mozart: K332, last movement, bb1–14

Here, the approach to V in b6 is, predictably enough, the supertonic chord of G, marked *. But its dominant-directional force is increased with a major third, B♮ (a temporary leading note), a seventh, F, and a minor ninth, A♭. It lacks the root G and is thus a 'diminished seventh'.

11.3   *The third-level dominant,* VI, is yet a third source of a diminished seventh chord. Again, it is a major chord with the root missing. In minor keys, its 5th needs raising with an accidental. An example is from *Die schöne Müllerin* no. IX, Ex. 11e.

Ex. 11e   'Des Müllers Blumen', *Die schöne Müllerin* no. IX, bb18–21

'Des Müllers Blumen', no. IX of Die schöne Müllerin, bb 18-21.

Here, b18 breaks into a dominant circle at III and reaches the next step, vi. b19 begins with VI which, with the root missing and the added ninth, G♮, is a diminished seventh. Regardless of its colouring (major and thickened with seventh and ninth) the chord behaves wholly predictably, continuing round the circle to ii, and thence to a slightly extended final perfect cadence.

Play this passage very slowly indeed, following in your mind the linear flow of each functioning note: observe major thirds rising, (E♯ to F♯, A♯ to B, etc.) and several sevenths and the minor ninth (G♮) all falling. Then play or listen to a recording, and sing, right through the song if you have it. You will notice that the last line of each verse is repeated and Schubert uses the richly coloured harmony to heighten the second emphatic singing of these final words.

11.4   The three diminished seventh chords, V$^{♭9}$ minus root, II$^{♭9}$ minus root and VI$^{♭9}$ minus root between them use up all the available twelve notes:

Ex. 11f

on C: V7   II7   VI7

In Chapter 15 we shall look further at how these chords can be remarkably ambiguous, acting between them as potential dominants of all twenty-four keys. For now, note only that *diminished sevenths are dominants* within the expanded meaning of 'dominant' which we are using throughout: their missing basses would want to fall a perfect fifth (or rise a fourth); their thirds rise as leading notes, real or temporary; their minor sevenths and minor ninths resolve down a semitone to the nearest available note in the next chord.

1.4.1   Now turn back to Ex. 11d where, at bb 12–14, analysis throws into relief some delightfully subtle yet powerfully directional harmony.

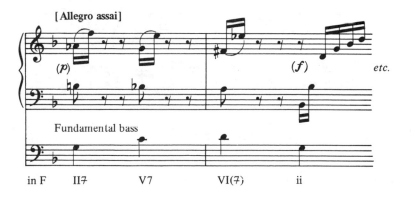

in F   II7   V7   VI(7)   ii

Play these two bars slowly and try to explain unaided the first three chords as they slide chromatically downwards. Your explanation should be along the following lines:

> Bb 12 and 13 contain two out of the three available diminished sevenths (though one note is missing from each chord). They actually disguise a segment of a circle of dominants interrupted by a substitute 'VI-not-I', as the fundamental bass analysis shows. The chain begins with II → V. Then, instead of the expected I, Mozart moves to VI (the F♯ temporary leading note of G major/minor gives us the visual clue), an 'interrupted' progression which allows another segment, → ii (→ V → I) to complete the musical phrase.

11.5   *Mental hearing and analysis exercise*
Read Ex. 11g, away from the keyboard. Begin with the left-hand triplet semiquavers which lend it some harmonic stability; then compile an aural image of the chromatic parallel sixths above. The example begins on the key centre of A minor.

Ex. 11g   Mozart: K576, third movement, bb87⁴–91¹

I = II

Next, play it several times, slowly,

(1) to confirm the accuracy of your reading; and
(2) to assist in an analysis of the last two bars.

Complete the fundamental bass and the numerical analysis beneath it. The essential point to recognise is, of course, that each diminished seventh is the highly coloured dominant of the following chord.

11.6   *Imitative exercise*
Rewrite Ex. 11h, 'Ach bleib bei uns', changing as many first- and second-level dominants into diminished sevenths as your taste will allow. While Bach may turn in his grave, you should acquire a facility in manipulating, and recognising the function and component thrusts of, this particular dominant variation. The first phrase is altered already, to serve as an example. Chords marked * are ripe for alteration, though you could abuse the chorale even further if you wish.

Ex. 11h Bach: R177, 'Ach bleib bei uns, Herr Jesu Christ'

In places, the melody will need alteration as well as the added lower parts.

.7 *Supplementary mental hearing and analysis exercise*
Alternately read and play, play and read, a phrase or two at a time, several of the songs in *Die schöne Müllerin*—or in *Winterreise* if your copy contains both of these Schubert song cycles. As you do so, note any diminished

sevenths: pause and examine which chords, V, II or VI, they are based on; see how they then behave 'dominantly', both as vertical structures implying resolution to their 'I/i's and as horizontal lines with leading notes, sevenths and minor ninths moving predictably up or down.

Note how often they are musical illuminations of a poet's meaning: the 'questioning' of *Die schöne Müllerin* no. VI is already evident in the raised eyebrow of bar two—a II-based diminished seventh before the voice has even begun to sing. The second bar of the opening *Winterreise* song, 'Gute Nacht', ends with a V-based diminished seventh, begun with a passionate appoggiatura in the upper part and poised over a repeated tonic pedal—a musical stress to match the verbal one in the following voice-part.

11.8   *Supplementary imitative exercise*
Take any phrases or longer passages which you came across while searching for diminished sevenths in 11.7 above. Copy the vocal line (cover up the piano part while your eye is so firmly glued to the original score) and then invent a piano accompaniment to it.

SUMMARY OF CHAPTER 11

(1) V+ minor seventh and ninth, with the root missing, is a 'diminished seventh'.
(2) So too are major II and VI, similarly coloured.
(3) (a) the 'leading' major third rises as ever;
    (b) the minor seventh falls as expected;
    (c) the minor ninth falls, too;
    (d) the fifths of II and VI need raising by an accidental in minor keys, to overcome the constraints of the key-signature.

CHAPTER 12

More Colourful Dominants: Augmented and Neapolitan Sixths

12.1 Another crop of colourful chords, best thought of as constructions on the second-level dominant, II, are the so-called augmented sixths.

12.1.1 The modifications to the diatonic chord are quite acute:

Ex. 12a

The third is sharpened to become major, and thus a temporary leading note which will rise.

The fifth is flattened to become diminished, and thus bound to resolve downwards, the shortest available distance.

The minor seventh is present, and naturally falls too.

The minor ninth is also included in one version and, of course, falls. as the semitone below is the nearest note in the following chord.

1.2 Augmented sixths are always in second inversion. Indeed, they *must* be to be so called: the crucial interval which gives them their name is (here) from A♭ to F♯, strongly dissonant and with an irresistible need to expand outwards to an octave.

1.3 There are three forms of the augmented sixth:

the Italian sixth reaching only to II⁷;
the French sixth (France is north of Italy) reaching further up to II⁸;

the German sixth (Germany stretches as far north as the Baltic) reaching up to $II^{\flat 9}$. (The mnemonic is ludicrous but effective.)

12.1.4   Like any other II, second-level dominant, chord, the augmented sixths always resolve to V in one form or another. Often the final V_3^5 is delayed: the German sixth in particular normally hangs on V_4^6 and avoids the parallel fifths $\left(\text{in } C, \dfrac{E\flat - D}{A\flat - G}\right)$ which are otherwise unavoidable.

12.3   THE ITALIAN SIXTH

Augmented sixths are almost unknown in Bach's chorale harmonisations (though 'Ich hab' mein Sach' Gott heimgestellt', R19, has one in b1). They are a regular part of the harmonic language of both Mozart and Schubert. Ex. 12b shows the barest, most 'southerly' kind, the Italian sixth:

Ex. 12b   Schubert: 'Wohin', *Die schöne Müllerin* no. II, bb38–9

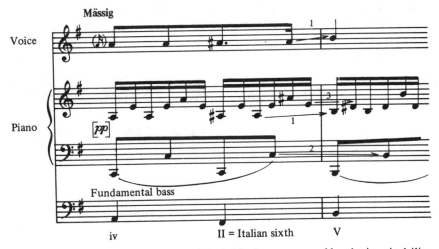

The 'II'-ness of the augmented sixth* is demonstrated by the inevitability of its resolution to the dominant:

the major third, A♯, rises to B;
the flattened fifth, C♮, falls to B;
the minor seventh, E♮, falls to D♯.

In a four-part chord this seventh is the note which would be doubled and would *rise* in one voice. The outward pull of the augmented sixth interval,

---

*The fact that the root, the supertonic note, is missing has led to much semantic argument about whether the Italian version of the augmented sixth is in fact a derivative of the supertonic chord. The outcome of such argument is quite irrelevant to our purposes: what matters is that the chord operates wholly predictably if you arbitrarily declare it to be a colourful version of the second-level dominant, of II^7. It progresses to V and all its constituent notes follow the demands which our ears make on them as parts of the major supertonic seventh chord.

here C♮—A♯, is so strong and inevitable that if anything is doubled it will be the seventh: measured against the gravitational pull of the other two notes, the seventh is now the *weakest* of the three and can stand one voice leaving it *upwards* while another resolves downwards.

2.3   THE FRENCH SIXTH

The inverted root of II appears as well as raised third, lowered fifth and minor seventh; it is less common than the Italian and German varieties. An example from Schubert is Ex. 12c:

Ex. 12c   Schubert: 'Pause', *Die schöne Müllerin* no. XII, bb39–41

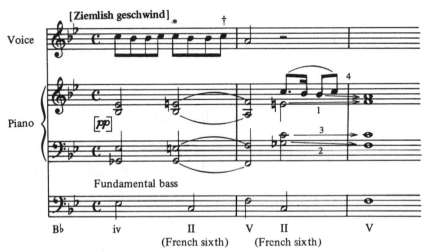

Here the voice first, then the piano, decorate the progression: the first augmented sixth could be analysed as no more than an Italian sixth decorated with appoggiatura (*) and échappée (+). The piano version, though, confirms the real French quality of the sustained 'tenor' C, the inversion of the (missing) root (marked 3).

Meanwhile:

(1) the major third 'leads' upwards,
(2) the tension of the flattened fifth is released downwards,
(4) the seventh, after escaping, finally responds to the ear's demand and falls.

Again, the 'II'-ness of the chord is clear both from its context (a substitute of the previous iv, strengthening the next step, a dominant stride to V), and also from the directional thrust of its constituent notes.

12.4   THE GERMAN SIXTH

This reaches higher still than the French, to the minor ninth. An example is from K332, Ex. 12d:

Ex. 12d   Mozart: K332, first movement, bb31–7

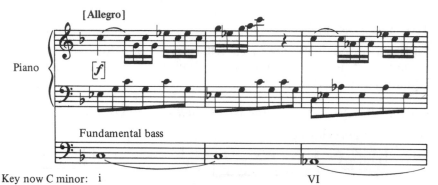

Key now C minor: i   VI

II (German sixth)   V

(This example follows immediately on from Ex. 11b. You could read them together if the whole sonata is not available to you).

Notice first the position of this coloured supertonic in the whole harmonic scheme:

> i falls to its substitute
> 'VI-not-i', generating the beginning of a dominant segment to
> II, the German sixth, leading as it must to
> V (which prepares the second subject in C major).

Secondly, notice the normality of the onward flow of the constituent notes. Even though this is a broad and arpeggiated piano texture,

(1a)   the temporary leading note, F♯, rises;

(1b)   in fact, its first appearance an octave lower is given a resolution too, in this case;

(2)   the lowered fifth releases its tension by moving to the nearest note available, down a semitone;

(3)   the seventh falls;

(4)   so does the minor ninth, making parallel fifths with the bass,
barely disguised by being arpeggiated. But there is no alternative if
the chord is to resolve at once to V_3^5.

5   These parallels are, however, avoided in a very common resolution of the
German sixth, to V_4^6. Many sonata movements of the classical period
display this vivid heightening of the harmonic colour approaching a
dominant before a second subject or towards the end of a movement. Look
at Ex. 12e:

Ex. 12e   Mozart: K533, Allegro, bb219–26[1]

Here are both examples of delaying resolution of II with V_4^6 instead of V_3^5 and also a remarkable demonstration of the relative intensity of coloured second-level dominants. Analyse it unaided, ignoring the fundamental bass, before reading on.

Analysis:

b219 is a major supertonic seventh, II^7c, with the root only touched on in passing in the right hand: dramatic enough, but outshone by
b221, a diminished seventh, again a supertonic chord, again without the security of more than passing reference to its root, and again eclipsed by
b223, the most brilliantly coloured, German sixth, version of the supertonic.

The enormous tension generated by these 'V-of-V's, and by their resolution to the irresolute $\frac{6}{4}$ form of V, is released only slowly: b225 breaks into the even faster right-hand notes of a trill, while the dominant chord begins with a suspended 4 → 3.

12.6   *Mental hearing and analysis exercises*
Read, analyse, memorise and write out Exs. 12f and 12g. Note particularly the contexts in which the colourful II chords are set and the normality with which each note in them resolves to V.

Ex. 12f   Schubert: 'Trockne Blumen', *Die schöne Müllerin*, no. XVIII, bb13–15

[Ziemlish langsam]

Ex. 12g   Mozart: K333, third movement, bb60–64

.7 *Imitative exercise*

Ex. 12h is the vocal line of a Schubert song, 'Das Sehnen'. Add a piano accompaniment, continuing the broken chord texture. At every opportunity to use II before V, ⁵₃ or ⁶₄, write an augmented sixth. In the first four bars, * marks points at which an augmented sixth is possible.

It may be helpful to remind yourself that:

(1) the tonic note is part of any augmented sixth;
(2) the supertonic note is part of a French sixth;
(3) the minor mediant note is part of a German sixth;
(4) the sharpened subdominant note is part of any augmented sixth.

The result of the exercise will *not* be Schubertian: you will, though, have gained considerable experience in manipulating these particular supertonic variants.

Ex. 12h   Schubert: 'Das Sehnen'

.8   THE NEAPOLITAN SIXTH

One more colourful variant of the second-level dominant remains. It was referred to in 4.4 as a chord based on a root which belongs to neither major nor minor mode, the flattened supertonic. Although ♭II is patently *not* dominantly related to V, an augmented fourth/diminished fifth away, the ear is prepared to pretend that it is so related. Just as we accept the distorted dominant relationship somewhere within a circle of fifths, (see Chapter 7.4 and following), so ♭II, in first inversion (it is a ⁶₃ chord, and so named

'Neapolitan *sixth*') is heard as a poignant *dominant* of V. Schubert uses it frequently, Ex. 12i:

Ex. 12i   Schubert: 'Der Müller und der Bach', *Die schöne Müllerin* no. XIX, bb7–10

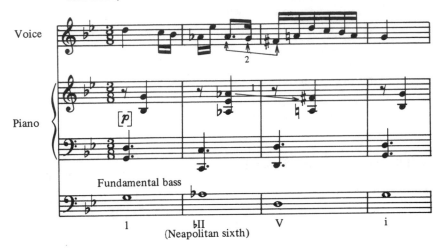

It belongs more comfortably in the minor mode: its fifth (here E♭) needs to be the *flattened* submediant. That apart, its use is straightforward: it replaces ii/II, and therefore aims most probably towards V, $^5_3$ or $^6_4$. The flattened supertonic note, of course, releases its tension by the shortest route, downwards to the leading note (marked '1'), sometimes passing via the tonic ('2').

12.9   *Mental hearing and analysis exercise*
Write several progressions, either copying them from examples you find in any music you have available, or inventing them yourself, on the progression i → ii/II → V → i. In each case, colour the second-level dominant. Use various forces and textures: four recorders, violin and piano, wind quintet and so on. Examples might include:

i → II⁷ → V → i;
I → ♭IIb (i.e. Neapolitan sixth) → V → i;
i → II♭⁵c (i.e. augmented sixth) → V → i.

Play them, memorise them, and play them again from memory. Sing each part as you play, identifying the horizontal flow generated by the gravitational pull of notes, particularly chromatically altered ones—the flat supertonic falling in a Neapolitan sixth, the sharpened subdominant rising in an augmented sixth, and so on.

12.10   *Supplementary mental hearing and analysis exercise*
Find, read, and memorise any of these more colourful dominants, first-, second- and third-level, in some or all of Schubert's *Die schöne Müllerin:*

no. V (piano introduction)
no. VI (piano introduction)
no. XV (bb1–12)
no. XVII (bb13–22)
no. XIX (bb60–70).

11   *Supplementary imitative exercise*
Write out the vocal line of the last three extracts listed above, and
recompose the piano accompaniment. If your memory serves you so well
that it is effectively copied, no harm is done. The aim is always to get as
close to the original as possible.

SUMMARY OF CHAPTER 12

(1) 'Augmented sixth' chords are best seen as supertonic chords with
sharp thirds, flat fifths and minor sevenths, in second inversion.

The 'Italian' sixth has only these three notes;
the 'French' sixth adds the inverted root;
the 'German' sixth adds the minor ninth.

(2) Like all supertonic chords, augmented sixths resolve most
convincingly to V ($\frac{5}{3}$ or $\frac{6}{4}\frac{5}{3}$).

(3) The 'Neapolitan sixth' is the sixth (i.e. $\frac{6}{3}$) chord on the *flat* supertonic.
It too resolves 'dominantly': ♭IIb → V ($\frac{5}{3}$ or $\frac{6\text{-}5}{4\text{-}3}$).

CHAPTER 13

Interlude IV: *More on Piano Textures*

13.1   In chorale harmonisations the directional flow of individual melodic lines is clearly visible. It is, too, in most of the textures created by several single-line instruments, though chords may be expanded upwards and downwards through a range much wider than that of the human voice, and chords are often extended in time, horizontally, by such devices as arpeggios and repeated broken chords. But it is in piano textures that the linear flow of parts can be most heavily disguised: the final resolution of a long scalar passage, or of arpeggios ranging widely over several octaves, may seem a long way from the expectations set up at the beginning of such figurations. The notation, too, is not easy to handle as so much material is contained within two staves. Even the draughtsmanship required for assembling notes in dense chords can be laborious and unwieldy.

These particular problems are coupled with the overwhelming importance of the piano as soloist, accompanist, concertist and partner in sonatas, trios and larger ensembles from the early classical period onwards. The efficient handling of piano textures is thus a skill which is an essential part of the analyst's tool-kit.

13.2   In fact, while piano textures are clearly less rigid in their linear demands than are the individual parts of vocal or single-line instrumental ensembles, the ear still demands that most expectations are realised; that at least one leading note of several at different octaves will rise; that at least the last seventh in a long scale will fall; that an augmented single-line instrumental ensembles, the ear still demands that most expectations are realised; that at least one leading note of several at different octaves will rise; that at least the last seventh in a long scale will fall; that an augmented sixth will finally expand outwards, even if it does so at an octave far removed from where it began.

13.3   To alert you to ways in which perfectly conventional progressions develop and resolve, disguised within these textures so different from four-part chords, the exposition of the first movement of Mozart's sonata, K547a, is annotated in Ex. 13a. It is Mozart's own transcription of K547, a sonata for violin and piano, and so demonstrates the piano as both soloist and accompanist.

Begin by reading the music away from the keyboard. As before, you will probably need to identify melodic phrases, partly memorise them, and build up a mental impression of their harmonic context. Take your time, and break the task up into manageable sections. Deal with only the first eight bars to begin with: the second eight are so similar that you will read them very much more quickly.

As the sounds begin to clarify off the page, notice the added reference numbers and, before reading the comments below to which they refer, try to anticipate the points to which they relate: making your own original analysis is a far more valuable exercise than simply reading that of someone else.

Ex. 13a Mozart: Sonata K547a, first movement, exposition

Bar

1   Where a chord is no more than a chord, its density and the amount of doubling it contains is entirely a matter of taste, colour and emphasis.

2   Returning notes, diatonic and chromatic, behave normally. The whole of this first three bars is the composing out of a single F major chord.

3   The piano can sustain coherent 'voices': this passage could be easily sung, or played by three single-line instruments. In such situations,

4   gravitational notes respond normally. Here, leading E♮ and V⁷ B♭ rise and fall respectively.

5   A common accompanying texture below I → V → I → V is a broken chord pattern reiterating the dominant note off the beat, as a pedal,

6   but, still, leading notes rise and

7   sevenths fall, even if the melody leads to the seventh, B♭, being omitted for a beat.

8   Octaves are a normal way of accentuating a melodic line even if the figuration is such that an octave texture can only be begun, not sustained. The first octaves appear with a *forte* dynamic;

9   the second octaves are an echoed repetition of the first, a kind of contradiction, a density associated with *forte* being here played captiously piano.

10   Octaves often strengthen the bass, too.

11   Scalar extensions of simple harmony begin and end on notes of the implied chord.

12   Adjacent chords are positively 'vocal' in their conformity.

13   Chromatic decorations resolve to their nearest neighbouring notes while,

14   added dominant sevenths fall as soon as the changing harmony allows. These four bars again use a dominant pedal; now the dominant note is in the middle of the texture, surrounded by returning notes and a developing harmonic bass.

15   To make a harmonic point, three notes may be needed in what begins (the second subject) as a single-line right-hand melody.

16   An arpeggiated chord both sustains a harmony through a length of time and also imparts a rhythmic pattern to it.

17   Oscillating octaves are a common pianistic device in either hand, and are the keyboard equivalent of the string tremolo. Here the harmonic structure is reversed, with the dominant note of the new key, common to both I and V⁷, sustained *above*

18   left-hand octaves for five emphatic beats. As the notes become too fast to be played in octaves within the limited technical demands of this style, octaves give way to single notes without breaking the continuity of the melodic line.

19   The structure reverts to melody on top, and the underlying harmony is sustained in one of the most common figurations of classical piano music,

20   the Alberti bass, rocking broken chords.

21   A dominant seventh an octave and a half above the starting point of the phrase finally resolves to the third of the (new) tonic. Did it not do so four bars earlier because all the aural attention was, here, focused on the opening of the right-hand melody?

22   onwards breaks the texture into two equally-weighted duos which reverse their roles at

23   Throughout, in a more contrapuntally conscientious passage, the gravitation needs of dissonant and leading notes are met with scrupulous care: at

24   begins a short sequence of diminished sevenths (VI⁷ → ii, V⁷ → I) every note of which is given its expected resolution.

25   The coda begins with another decoration of a sustained pedal, the new tonic, C.

26   extends the C chord through two bars, first with a rising scale and secondly with a scale falling at half the pace because each note is interrupted by an échappée.

27   The final inflexion of the added seventh (B♭) resolves, after the last échappée, to A, while arpeggiated chords,

28   similarly disguise careful resolutions of the dominant third and seventh.

13.4   After such an aural and analytical investigation, try some imitative exercises in which you apply these kinds of texture and figuration to some pastiche of your own. For example, write half-a-dozen eight-bar variations based on the second subject of this sonata (bb32–9). Some openings might be:

SUMMARY OF CHAPTER 13

(1) Neither expansion nor decoration of a chord into a characteristic piano texture reduces the gravitational pull of notes which have such an impulse to resolve.
These are:

> leading notes,
> added sevenths and ninths,
> suspensions and appoggiaturas,
> auxiliary, or returning, and passing notes.

(2) Where the texture is expanded over several octaves, such resolutions may not be at the same octave as that at which the tension was initiated.

(3) Doublings of 'leading' thirds and dissonances can occur freely in expanded keyboard textures such as arpeggios and scales, and in dense chords of 5 or 6 notes or more.

(4) Common piano figurations and textures include:

> broken chords and Alberti bass
> octave reinforcement
> octave oscillations
> off-beat repetitions of dominant notes within a harmonic progression
> arpeggios and extended scales beginning and ending on harmony notes.

CHAPTER 14

Irresolute Progressions, Episodic Six-threes, Reverse Thrust and Pedals

14.1   By now it will be clear that in the core texts we are using and, in fact, in tonal music for a further hundred years or more, a large proportion of harmonic relationships are achieved through the dominant urge to resolve to the tonic. Chapters 4, 5, 7 and 8 stretched this concept by analogy to second-, third- and further-level dominants and finally all the way round a complete circle of fifths. Chapters 11 and 12 stressed the same dominant principle driving every chromatically altered chord to its resolution. Chapter 10 maintained the same principle but introduced alternative ways in which dominant tension can be released, into *substitute* resolutions.

The only progression so far which has had nothing to do with 'dominant' forces is that from a chord to its substitute *statement* (10.3.2. and 10.6).

The present chapter investigates this further, together with some other ways in which harmony sustains forward momentum without the help of dominants. Note, though, that this is much rarer than dominant-driven harmony: the forces described in Chapter 2 remain the principal source of harmonic impetus in tonal music.

14.2   OSCILLATIONS

Occasionally harmony will oscillate between chords which are potential 'substitutes' of each other, chords a third apart. Surprisingly this is true of the opening of some chorale harmonisations, despite the density and intensity of their normally dominant-powered harmony. It is as if Bach were avoiding, unexpectedly, a declaration of key in contrast to his normal practice of announcing tonality unequivocally. While the largest majority of Bach's chorale harmonisations begin with I/i → V or V → I/i, some begin with vi → Ib or i → IIIb. Examine Exs. 14a and 14b.

Ex. 14a   Bach: R336, 'Wo Gott der Herr', b1

? $\begin{cases} b \\ D \end{cases}$ $\begin{matrix} i \\ vi \end{matrix}$ $\begin{matrix} IIIb \\ Ib \end{matrix}$ IV $\begin{matrix} \\ Ib \end{matrix}$ [= b]

Ex. 14b   Bach: R341, 'Ich dank' dir', b1

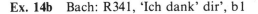

? $\begin{cases} f\sharp \\ A \end{cases}$ $\begin{matrix} i \\ vi \end{matrix}$ $\begin{matrix} IIIb \\ Ib \end{matrix}$ I   IV   [= A]

Is R336 in D major (beginning vi → Ib) or in b minor (beginning i → IIIb)? Is R341 in A major (beginning vi → Ib) or in f♯ (beginning i → IIIb)? There is no way of telling: at such moments, Bach chooses to leave the question unanswered in a brief irresolute moment. (In fact, R336 begins with i; it ends in b minor: R341 begins with vi; the last phrase ends in A major.)

4.3   The irresolute nature of substitutes, their inability to define the whereabouts of a tonic, becomes even more marked when one substitute melts in turn into another. We noted a chain of them in chapter 10 (Ex. 10i) and that same chain, R158, contrasts extraordinarily with another one, R160. They are Exs. 14c and 14d respectively.

Ex. 14c   Bach: R158, 'Der Tag, der ist so freudenreich'

I   vi   IV   (ii)

Ex. 14d   Bach: R160, 'Gelobet seist du'

V   iii   I   (IV)

The only aural clue to the key of Ex. 14c is the F♯ passing note from the first chord. Ex. 14d could as easily also be interpreted aurally as G major: it opens with an irresolute episode of three chords before an F♮ gives our ears a clue to define the key. In fact, the ambiguity which this particular substitute chain imparts reflects the nature of the chorale melody. 'Gelobet seist du' is modal and begins and ends on the dominant (in what is known as the 'plagal' version of the mode) rather than on the tonic (the 'authentic' version).

The point for our purposes is that substitutes, and particularly chains of them, can produce a state of harmonic suspended animation, compared with the energetic purposefulness of harmony driven on by 'dominant' forces.

14.4   For a brief aural, analytical and imitative exercise in passing, read and analyse Ex. 14e, the opening phrase of 'Verleih' uns Frieden gnädiglich', without the help of an instrument.

Ex. 14e   Bach: R91, 'Verleih' uns Frieden gnädiglich', bb1–2

It begins in f♯ minor, i → VI → iv⁷ → etc.

Now copy out the first three chords, but continue by inventing the end of a phrase in A major (with an E♮). The opening three chords will now imply vi → IV →ii⁷ → etc.

14.5   PARALLEL SIX-THREES

We investigated in Chapter 8 ways in which music can be extended by dominant-powered episodic excursions. Another frequent episodic device is a row of first inversions, a scale of ⁶₃s, with no dominant implications at all.

The device works because a scale is musically so powerful and directional.

As

is a coherent musical line flowing melodically from submediant to tonic of D major, so it can be enriched with parallel lines beneath it:

It is then open to all kinds of decoration: this very row of $^6_3$ chords appears twice in succession in the first movement of K283, decorated differently each time.

Ex. 14f Mozart: K283, first movement, bb45–51

The first decoration is by a series of 7 → 6 suspensions, the '6' of each chord held up for a quaver as the '7' of the next. The second decoration is more florid with accented passing notes and chromatic appoggiaturas disclosing a potential of which the first two bars gave no clue.

Alternately read, play and read this example until the sound is securely locked in your mind. You might then invent a couple of further decorated versions: try adding chromatic downward auxiliary notes to the top line—BA♯B, AG♯A, etc.—or convert the progression into a single broken line for recorder or violin—DF♯BD, C♯EAC♯, etc.

4.6   This 'parallel stepwise $^6_3$' device can also be used upwards. In the last movement of the same sonata, Mozart writes:

Ex. 14g   Mozart: K283, Presto, bb9–13

Play this through once or twice, and then extend the same pattern upwards: Vb → vib → viib → Ib →iib → etc. You will find that episodes like this need a secure starting and finishing point. Ex. 14f ended on I, Ex. 14g ended on V. Strong props are needed to support the harmonically weak episode hanging between them.

14.7   *Mental hearing and analysis exercise*
Read, unaided at first and then confirmed by playing if you are not confident of the accuracy of your reading, Ex. 14h.

Ex. 14h   Mozart: K533, Allegro, bb57–61

Now, before looking at the specimen answer below, make an analysis of the harmony, noting particularly where it is episodic and where it is strongly driven by the thrust of dominant-related chords.
Your analysis may read something like this:

Key now C major/minor.
b57:   descending scale of C ending on a diminished seventh chord derived from II^{b9}, resolving normally to

b58:	V(b) with an appoggiatura in the melody and an anticipatory note ending each group of three quavers. This bar, however, continues with harmonically episodic parallel $^6_3$ chords—IVb → iiib → iib to
b59	Ib. The descending scale of b57 reappears, now minor and in the left hand. It too ends on a $II^{b\circ}$ diminished seventh resolving to
b60:	V, with an appoggiatura and an escaping anticipation on either side of the harmonic G, and a 4–3 suspension above. Now, however, the figure is extended *not* with episodic $^6_3$s but harmonised dominantly: V^7d → Ib → V^7 c/b, → Ia. (In each chord, appoggiaturas and/or anticipations colour the simple harmony described.)
Conclusion:	the passage consists of two pairs of bars. The first pair contain a musical extension of parallel stewpwise $^6_3$ between two strong tonic points. In the second pair, the same musical material is developed and strengthened by being harmonised by the two most powerfully related chords, I and V^7.

4.8 *Imitative exercise*
Add a simple left-hand part to this melody. Use only i, V with various levels of added sevenths and ninths, variants of II^7, and a row of parallel $^6_3$s. (Although the key-signature shows it to be part of a movement in F major, this particular passage is in c minor.)

For the working which is self-evidently perfect Mozart, now turn to K332, the last movement, bb50–65.

4.9 *Supplementary mental hearing and analysis exercise*
Search for, analyse, memorise and write out more passages including strings of $^6_3$ chords moving by step. You will find one at the end of the bridge passage of K576, the first movement. Find some more in Mozart's sonatas; they are not characteristic of the more urgent harmony of Bach chorales or of the purposeful vocal phrases of *Die schöne Müllerin*.

14.10   *Supplementary imitative exercises*

Write some pastiche passages in the style of Mozart, for piano or for solo instrument with piano accompaniment. Plan them out keeping in mind the need for a coherent harmonic rhythm: change chords on strong beats, arrive at points of repose after two or four bar phrases and avoid reaching cadences too soon or too late, so contradicting the natural growth of classical phrases in pairs of bars, or four or eight, but not in less predictable lengths.

Such a scheme as I | I | vi II | V | vib Vb | IVb iiib | iib Ib | V would make eight bars which could be composed out into something along the lines of Ex. 14i:

Ex. 14i

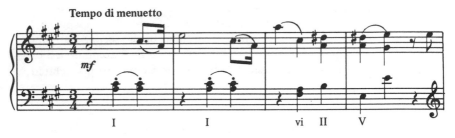

A first step might be no more than to repeat the whole eight bars, changing only the final cadence from imperfect (I → V) to perfect (V → I). This would also inhibit you from creating too much new music. Mozart, like most exceptional composers, uses remarkably little material: it is its quality and the way in which he expands it which expose his imagination and craftsmanship.

14.11   REVERSE THRUSTS

The most powerful, and most common, harmonic progressions we have examined have been *from* dominant *to* tonic. This includes equivalent progressions too: *from* II (= V of V) *to* V; *from* V *to* vi (= substitute for I). The thrust of such progressions is reversible. Two examples are common:

14.11.1   *from* I *to* V. The tonic, standing as it does at the very centre of the harmonic universe, can be a starting point for a *reversed* dominant thrust. This is very common indeed, the most frequent opening of all harmonic spans. Analyse the opening two chords of some Mozart sonata movements—or some Beethoven quartets, some Brahms songs or anything else you may have available which uses the conventions of tonal harmony.

In fact the tonic, and it alone, can be the starting point of *any* size of step:

thus I → ii is the 'interrupted' I → IV dominant progression
    I → iii is a substitute statement
    I → IV is a 'dominant' resolution
    I → V is the dominant progression in reverse
    I → vi is another substitute statement
    I → vii(b) is I → V with a substitute resolution

To define the first step of a harmonic expedition, any progression from I is viable. It is only after this first outward step has been taken that the urge to return home is expressed, so often in dominant strides.

.11.2   Another 'reverse thrust' is that *from* IV *to* I. As an ending it is common enough to merit a name, the 'plagal' cadence. Bach uses it occasionally: in the chorale harmonisations it several times appears as a kind of harmonic coda, extending the time-span of what begins as a perfect cadence, but with V followed by the less assertive first inversion of I before this brief glimpse of the 'anti-dominant' side (see 7.13), Ex. 14j:

Ex. 14j   Bach: R143, 'In dulci jubilo', bb29–32

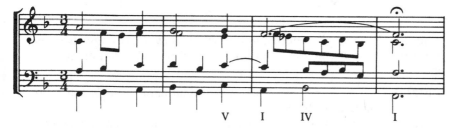

Occasionally, too, IV → I may occur during a phrase. Where it does so it can produce a considerable sense of instability; Ex. 14k shows it at a moment when a tonal centre of A major is being disturbed (G♮) with little indication of another secure centre until the cadence a bar later.

Ex. 14k   Bach: R336, 'Wo Gott der Herr', bb1–4

(This instability sustains the remarkably insecure opening of this chorale, discussed above at 13.2.)

14.11.3   Further reversals of the 'dominant-to-its-tonic' progression are rare. Where they do occur they often imply a new beginning, the break between one phrase and the next. They are so contrary in function to V → I, ii → V etc. that they imply the opposite of the forward drive inherent in dominants. An example appears in 'Die böse Farbe', no. XVII of *Die schöne Müllerin:*

Ex. 141   Schubert: 'Die böse Farbe', *Die schöne Müllerin* no. XVII, bb 15–18

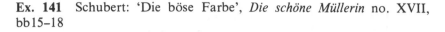

Read it and analyse the chords, noting where they imply commas in the forward flow of the music. Your analysis will probably run along these lines:

b15–16[1]: vi → V → I → V; a conventional enough approach to an imperfect cadence.

b16[2]–16[3]: II → V: a kind of harmonic coda, a reinforcement of V created by a perfect cadence on it.

b17–18[1]: ii: ii *after* V clearly implies the beginning of a *new* phrase. It is not really a V → ii progression at all, but a halt on V, a comma in the vocal line, and a new phrase of, conventionally, ii → V → i.

14.12   Play for yourself I → V → ii → vi (→ iii → vii → IV → I). It has an unstable, searching quality about it and is difficult to conceive of as a continuous harmonic flow. Instead, it sounds like a series of first steps, a sequence of 'I → V's, and the distorted interval, the diminished fifth/augmented fourth, is certainly not acceptable to the ear as a dominant distance in reverse (c.f. 7.4). You will find no examples of reversed dominant thrust reaching anywhere near this extreme within our three core texts though composers in other idioms than these do hit on longer chains of the searching progression: the song 'Hey Joe', written by B. Roberts in 1968 and sung and played by Jimi Hendrix begins C → G → D → A → E. Listen, and look, for more as you experience any music on radio, record or tape, or as you make it yourself.

.13 PEDALS

One more harmonic phenomenon, referred to in passing in 2.4.2 (4) and
elsewhere, is the 'pedal'. The name is derived from organ music in which the
player's foot holds a sustained note while the hands play changing
harmony above. Pedal notes are almost invariably either tonic or
dominant, and *neither imposes any restriction at all on the harmony above:* as
far as accurate grammatical harmony is concerned, ignore the sustained
bass note.

Consider the opening of 'Pause', Ex. 14m:

Ex. 14m   Schubert: 'Pause', *Die schöne Müllerin no. XII, bb1–4*

The chord marked * is a harmonic nonsense in isolation—play it alone, out
of context—but the (spread) cluster of notes, G + A + Bb + C (+ Eb) is
perfectly comprehensible to the ear which hears a dominant ninth with the
root, F, missing, above a tonic pedal note, Bb.

Pedals have the effect of *weakening the security of harmony* by adding
dissonance while *strengthening the hold of tonality* by maintaining a grasp
on one or other of the central notes, tonic and dominant.

.14 *Mental hearing and analysis exercise*
Read and hear, unaided by an instrument, the opening of 'Der Müller und
der Bach', Ex. 14n. Then write it out from memory, explaining bb4 and 5.

Ex. 14n   Schubert; 'Der Müller und der Bach', *Die schöne Müllerin* no.
XIX, bb1–6

14.15   *Imitative exercise*

Written sequences of strongly directional chords (say I → V → I → ii → V → I or i → V → i → Neapolitan IIb → V → i) over a tonic pedal and a dominant pedal. The result may be more violent than Schubert would have conceived, but the exercise should free you of inhibitions in the writing of crashing dissonances.

SUMMARY OF CHAPTER 14

(1) Harmonic progress is sometimes suspended by progressions which, while aurally acceptable, do not have a strong gravitational attraction through 'dominant' relationship. These include:

(a) oscillations between, or chains of, chords which are related as 'substitutes', standing a third apart from each other;
(b) rows of parallel first inversions, ⁶₃s, both downwards and upwards.

(2) the 'dominant-to-tonic' thrust can be reversed. I/i to V is common: reversing at deeper levels is less frequent. It often implies a breach of harmonic continuity.

(3) Pedals (normally tonic or dominant notes) can be ignored in harmonic analysis and construction, though their aural effect is powerful and, at times, intensely dissonant.

CHAPTER 15

Harmonic Puns and
Further Modulations

15.1   In Chapter 11, diminished sevenths were analysed as 'dominant minor ninths with the roots missing' on the first-level dominant (11.1), the second-level dominant (11.2) and the third-level dominant (11.3). However, a phenomenon of the diminished seventh is that it remains the same however much it is inverted, whichever way you look at it or listen to it. This must be so as its notes are an infinitely repeating pile of minor thirds. It follows, therefore, that it is a chord particularly prone to double meaning, to the musical pun, as *any one of its notes can be the leading note of a subsequent chord.* Look at Ex. 15a:

Ex. 15a

The chord marked 1 is the diminished seventh created out of the 'dominant minor ninth with the root missing' of C major: the fundamental bass proves it, and it resolves accordingly with the leading note, B, rising to C (and seventh, F, and ninth, A♭, falling). But chord 2 proves, equally conclusively, that the same notes, spelled differently, are the 'dominant minor ninth with the root missing' of E♭: the leading note, D, rises to E♭ and seventh and ninth, A♭ and C♭, fall.

The same reasoning makes chord 3 the dominant of F♯ and chord 4 the dominant of A. Follow the reasoning through for yourself: what is the leading note and does it rise? What notes are seventh and ninth respectively and do they fall?

Extemporise at the keyboard a couple of chords with which to approach the first diminished seventh and then experiment with the four routes out of it, each to either major or minor mode tonics: there are eight tonic

133

resolutions of a diminished seventh. The more remote exits will come as a shock until you have made them predictable simply by repeating them.

There can be only three diminished sevenths (re-read 11.4) and between them they can reach $3 \times 8 = 24$ tonics, the whole spectrum of major and minor keys in tonal harmony.

15.2   Not surprisingly, in our three core texts you will not find examples of such violent changes of direction. It is not part of Mozart's style to enter a diminished seventh from C and leave it into F♯. Diminished seventh puns, double meanings, do however serve as the means of more predictable changes of tonal direction. Consider by reading, then playing to confirm your reading accuracy, and finally analysing the harmonic functioning of, Ex. 15b:

Ex. 15b

Clearly, after a broken chord of A♭ comes an extended $V^{♭9}_7$, a diminished seventh; the leading note is G, the seventh D♭ and the ninth F♭. It will resolve back to A♭ as suggested in the chord in brackets.

In fact, Mozart (it is bb16–18 of the *più allegro* passage in the Fantasia, K475) spells the F♭ as an E♮, Ex. 14c: the diminished seventh, entered as V of A♭ is left as V of f (minor actually, though either mode is accessible from the 7 chord).

Ex. 15c   Mozart: K475, Più allegro, bb16–18

(Mozart actually extends the V for a further two bars before resolving onto i, f minor, at b21.)

15.3   As an exercise in manipulation, though not in stylish Mozartian pastiche, rewrite the last two chords of Ex. 15c so that

(a) the B♭ becomes, as A♯, the leading note of B major/minor and

(b) the D♭ becomes, as C♯, the leading note of D major/minor.

You may find it helpful to identify the minor ninth and make it fall first. For example the penultimate chord of Ex. 15c looks more unequivocally 'dominant' if it is given a root somewhere within its dense texture, as in Ex. 15d:

Ex. 15d

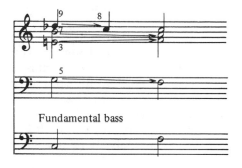

5.4   The augmented sixths also serve at times as dominant puns. Most commonly this device consists of treating as an augmented sixth what is first *heard* (not written) as a probable V⁷. Consider, (read, play and analyse), Ex. 15e.

Ex. 15e   Schubert: 'Mein!', *Die schöne Müllerin* no. XI, bb58–64

Clearly, as this passage begins, the tonal centre is B♭ (and has been since b39, long enough to convince our ears that the music is in the *key* of B♭). At b61 our ears observe the adding of an A♭ to the tonic chord: creating a V⁷, a dominant at one level or another, is such a common process in Schubert's language that this is surely our first interpretation of the sound of b61. Our eyes, however, tell us differently. By spelling A♭ as G♯ Schubert writes not a dominant seventh but an augmented sixth. This then resolves normally to V (⁶₄ then ⁵₃) of d minor, ready for a 'tierce de Picardie' to return to D major in b64.

All this, of course, is analysis on the small scale. In the larger context of the whole song (play it on piano or record and sing as you play) D major is the security which is sought for: the pun is not a musical aberration but a subtle though no less welcome return to the opening key.

15.2   *Mental hearing and analysis exercise*
Read, confirm by playing, and explain to yourself how Ex. 15f steers a course from G major to b minor. Only after doing this should you look at the specimen answer below.

Ex. 15f   Mozart: K475, bb22–3

Specimen analysis:

b21:   manifestly the composing out of the chord of G major, to which the ear may well hear

b22:   the addition of a seventh, F♮. The A♯ in the inner part is no more than a chromatic returning note, but the C♯ two notes later, retained throughout the bar, has no place in G⁷₃: the heard F♮ *must* therefore be an E♯, and the chord is that rich variant of II, an augmented sixth.

b23:   Predictably, this II proceeds to V and thence to i of b minor.

15.6 Another pun characteristic of Mozart at his more fanciful and towards the end of his short life is the single–note root of a dominant which becomes the third of the following chord. Here for once dominants are not the principal force involved. Indeed the device *weakens* a dominant. Consider Ex. 15g from that most productive, and exceptional, Fantasia K475 which introduces the sonata K457. (Play the whole work, now if you have it, or as soon as you can lay hands on a copy and/or a recording.)

Ex. 15g Mozart: K475, b25⁴–27²

Here, the root of the F♯ major, V of b minor, hangs poised in mid-air, repeated four times, until it suddenly changes its mood and character to become part of a chord, D major, unexpected but related: D is the relative major of b.

Seek out other examples of this musical pun. Many major-key opera arias from Handel and other late baroque composers make their 'da capo' return like this; Elgar reaches 'Nimrod' in the same way in the Enigma Variations—a G root becomes the third of E♭.

15.7 *Supplementary mental hearing and analysis exercise*
Read, with as little external help as possible consistent with achieving success in 'hearing' it accurately, the slow movement, Adagio, of the Sonata K457 which follows the Fantasia. At one point Mozart again makes the root of a V into the third of an unexpected new I. Identify it. (It is actually between bars 31 and 32, decorated with lower and upper returning notes—but search for it aurally rather than giving up and counting bar numbers.)

15.8 The extraordinarily chromatic Fantasia K475, perhaps the movement in all these keyboard works which offers most reward to the analyst, provides an example of another pun. It is rare and far-fetched in Mozart's style, but worth noting for its originality. It is part of what, in Chapter 8, was described as an excursion, but exceptionally extreme and involving a change in 'spelling' as C♭ becomes B♮.

Ex. 15h   Mozart: Fantasia K475, bb8–11[1]

In the context, now established, of eb minor, bar 10 clearly begins as VI, an interrupted cadence, Cb as a substitute for i, eb. Then the chord takes on a new and more central guise; the added major seventh, A♯, first alerts the ear to something unusual going on. The following V⁷ proves, in retrospect, that Cb (or B♮) has now become I.

Look further into the surrounding bars if you have the piece: this startling change of course proves to be only one step in an extraordinarily wide-ranging scheme of momentary tonics.

15.9   By now it will be clear that the principles that

(1) any major chord can be a dominant, and
(2) 'dominants' occur at several levels, deeper than only the final approach to a tonic,

allow various other puns and sudden changes of harmonic direction.

The Neapolitan sixth, the first inversion of bII (see 12.8) can be the dominant of the remotest key. Try c minor → Db⁶₃ → Gb major! In this progression the Db⁶₃ could be a second-level dominant so that not one but two steps take the harmonic construction *through* Gb[⁷] to Cb (call it B) major. One more step and Db is the *third*-level dominant towards E major.

Or any of these chords except the penultimate may be minor; only the final dominant needs the positive assertion of a major third as a definitive leading note.

Such extremes, however, are rarer and belong to the more chromatic dialect of later romantic music. They belong in the vocabulary of Liszt, Wagner and Richard Strauss rather than of Bach, Mozart and Schubert, and are thus beyond our self-imposed limits. Be alert though to their possibilities as you apply the analytical tool of harmonic dissection to later tonal music. As with composers as unalike as Bach and Schubert, the harmonic principles are universal: it is their proportions, the density of dissonance and the pace and stability of key-centres which vary.

15.10   MODULATION

One concept which has been frequently referred to, glossed over, and never fully explained is that of modulation. Its meaning is simple: it refers to the moving of the key-centre from one place to another (1.12.). What is difficult is to decide exactly when a modulation has actually occurred.

There is precedent from some theorists for considering that every momentary 'tonic' resolution of a passing 'dominant' at the second-level, the third-level or beyond is a brief modulation.

Alternatively, after say the 78-bar exposition of K547a (Ex. 13a), when the music has clearly travelled from F to C, no more than a direct return to the opening is needed, as demanded by the repeat sign, to be still 'in F major'. Continue into the development, however, and there is equally no doubt that the music is 'in C' even though we retain enough memory of F to feel that this C is at the same time a staging post, a temporary refuge, rather than a permanent home.

15.11   So, begging the semantic question of 'when is a modulation?', we can still clearly recognise that key-centres will be displaced both momentarily and also in the long term.

15.12   Key-centres can move as the result of three kinds of harmonic process:

15.12.1   A 'pivot' chord may be common to two key-centres. Most often this will be a major chord in the centre to be abandoned which is then seen to be the dominant of the new key. Look back to 5.6 and Ex. 5e where

(1) I of B was deemed to be V of *e*, the most direct of modulations. Then
(2) i of e was deemed to be ii of D, (followed by V and I). Then
(3) III of D was deemed to be V of b.

In the course of a classical exposition, you will often come across a *third-*level dominant, VI, resolving to the second-level, II, before it in turn arrives finally at the dominant key. This extra step helps to stabilise the new key, to make it appear like a real tonic rather than a passing reference to V, too easily restorable to I to be a convincing modulation. Ex. 15i shows this clearly:

Ex. 15i Mozart: K333, first movement, exposition

The key is B♭ major.

b12:   E♮ makes its appearance, V of V.

bb15–16: B♮ gives a warning of its appearance, a mere chromatic returning note.

b17:   B♮ now appears as a genuine harmonic element, VI = V of V of V.

b21:   The cancellation of B♮ makes the final arrival at V of V (b22) a *return* to relative security rather than a groping step into the unknown. The territory of 'C = V of F' has already been explored and charted; it is familiar ground so that

b23:   the second subject is securely *in* a new tonic, F, major, rather than *on* the dominant of the original B♭.

15.12.2   A single 'pivot' note may be common to two otherwise more or less unrelated chords. Look again at Ex. 15g. Mozart achieved the striking step into unexpectedly new territory here by what was described as a musical pun: F♯ = the root of F♯ and the third of D. The gulf between the two key centres was bridged by repeating the one note common to both chords.

15.12.3   The third means of modulation, somewhat rarer, at least within the styles of our core texts, is by 'assertion'. A chord is arrived at and arbitrarily declared to be a new tonic. Ex. 15h shows a case in point: B major is *not* a tonic until the following F♯^{7}, the dominant, asserts that it *is,* whatever our ears may have insisted to the contrary.

15.13   In the process of harmonic and tonal analysis, it is best to *minimise the concept of modulation.* Avoid the notion that every chromatic alteration implies moving *into* a new key. Often, it signifies no more than moving *onto* a temporary 'dominant' at one level or another. The wood of a larger harmonic framework is easily obscured by the trees of momentary chromaticisms and steps onto dominant circles, segments, excursions or episodes.

15.14   *Mental hearing and analysis exercise*
Read, unaided and then confirming by playing, either live or from a recording, Ex. 15i above. Now make a detailed analysis of it, searching out all the points you have covered throughout the book. Glance through, but do not read in enough detail to memorise, the specimen analysis below. Then attempt to make your own.

Specimen analysis

(1) *Overall tonal framework upon which the musical material is hung:* what are the key centres?

KEY B♭
b1: B♭
KEY F?
b12:   = II (= ?V) of F, but how easily could B♭ be confirmed if b14 included an E♭. Play it!)
KEY F CONFIRMED

b17: step to a further level of dominant, VI, confirming that now the tonality has shifted up a level. I = F, V = C, and this G

b18⁴+ now = II.

19: B♮ now cancelled, stepping back into well-charted new tonality of F ready for

b23: second subject, conventionally *in* the dominant key. Thence all sentences begin and end in F.

bb23–38: have brief tentative steps further back through dominants (B♮s in b25 and b33) but there is no modulation.

bb39–50: reaching further. B44 = III$^{♭9}$ → vi (→ ii → V → I). B47; VI – ii (– V – I). Again there is no modulation.

KEY F?

bb50–63: allude frequently to the original key with E♭s suggested and then rejected. The security of F is being questioned and, as the repeat is played,

KEY B♭

b1 returns, with no need of any harmonic contrivances, to B♭ while, the second time the exposition is played,

KEY F

b64 continues equally confidently in F.

(2) *Harmonic thrust:* what are the component forces?

bb1–4: powerful (I →) vi → ii → V → I.

b5: less pressing harmony of parallel ⁶₄s.

bb11–14: slower and more stolid dominant related I → II → V (= new I?) at a point where the tonal stability is threatened but

bb15–17: unequivocal dominant-related harmony changing every half-bar.

etc. . . . .

(3) *Relate these harmonic discoveries to phrase-structure:* how do the pace and placing of one influence the other?

bb1–2: a two-bar half-phrase above I → V.

bb3–4: a complementary half-phrase, the melody using the same rhythm, over complementary V → I.

etc. . . . .

(4) *Consider the functions and proportions of all melody notes:* how do they create a coherent line?

b0⁴: appoggiatura falling to strong dominant note, passing to continuing downward scale but

b1¹: arriving on a note above the harmonised tonic, allowing a longer appoggiatura, C to B♭.

etc. . . . .

(5) *Consider the function of all accompanying notes:* how do they sustain a harmonic and rhythmic flow and create a diversity of textures?

b1–5:   characteristic piano pattern of broken chords, the first note of each announcing its harmonic intention and the remainder sustaining a quaver flow in an 'alto/tenor' middle register.

b6:   silence after Ib has been asserted by the first two-note chord so far in the left hand.

etc. . . . .

You will clearly *not* want to analyse in such detail as (3), (4) and (5) throughout, but the ability to do so is a vital tool for analysing particularly striking moments of music you hear or, perhaps, for deciphering the underlying processes in a particular fragment of a piece you are learning to play. Such 'total analysis' is also an invaluable aid to memorising for a performer. How much can you remember now after doing the exercise?

15.15   *Imitative exercise*
Write a comparable exposition, clinging tenaciously to the style, the harmonic pace and thrust, the tonality, the melodic phrase-lengths and the textures, but inventing your own material.

15.16   Supplementary mental hearing, analysis and imitative exercises are now limitlessly available to you and each one will develop new levels of awareness, new measures of comparison for the next. At first keep fairly close to the styles of the core texts with which you will now be familiar. Try your hand at investigating a string quartet movement by Haydn or from Beethoven's Op. 18. Consider a Schumann *Lied* or a Mendelssohn 'Song without Words'. Eventually, though, the underlying harmonic principles will serve as the basis for analysis of any music conceived within the framework of tonal harmony from the latter part of the sixteenth century to much of the art music, and some of the 'pop' music, of the present day.

SUMMARY OF CHAPTER 15

(1) Any note of a diminished seventh may be treated as a leading-note for the purpose of resolving the chord. Thus each 7 leads to four keys each in two modes. So between all three 7s access can be gained to all 24 keys in the tonal system. Changes of 'spelling' may be required to retain coherent notational symbols of the enharmonic processes involved.

(2) Augmented sixths can also be 'spelled' differently, as minor sevenths with access to the most extreme key in a single step.

(3) Single notes may begin as one harmonic concept and become another.

(4) As any major chord can be left as a dominant, 'first-level' or further round the dominant-relating circle, this must include such foreign chords as the Neapolitan sixth.

(5) A modulation needs decisive *retrospective confirmation* after the *prospective possibility* of its existence has been declared by a harmonic progression.

Modulations can be achieved by:

   (a) 'Pivot' chords', common to both the key abandoned and the new key;
   (b) 'Pivot notes', common to two chords which may otherwise be unrelated by any gravitational pull;
   (c) 'Assertion', where a completely foreign chord is thrust into the position of being a new tonic by its dominant implying that there is no musical alternative to be understood by the ear.

CHAPTER 16

Further Exploration

The previous chapters have been designed to develop various skills and clarify various concepts. Your ability to read silently, to conceptualise the sounds implied by the symbols, should be greater, though you should not expect to pick up a score and read it fluently and up to speed unless you have an aural imagination granted to few.

Part of this skill will stem from an awareness of what is most likely to be happening in the music you read. Indeed, a familiarity with the style of both a period of music and a particular composer within it helps this reading ability enormously: as with reading prose, the less each letter, each word, needs to be consciously absorbed, assessed and interpreted, the more will speed and fluency increase.

So, to apply your reading ability to a previously unfamiliar style, you should begin by making it more familiar with extensive listening. After a diet of *Die schöne Müllerin,* the notation of the songs of Hugo Wolf or Mussorgsky will seem to disguise heavily their dominant thrust. Steep yourself in their sound for a while, and they will become much more accessible to eye and mental ear.

Associated with this reading ability is a skill of particular value to performers—memorising. Some depend on finger memory, a kind of automatic muscular reaction to each particular musical situation. Some play 'by ear', having taught their fingers to make the sounds their minds imagine. Others have a photographic memory, using the printed notes even when they are not physically present. For all, a recognition of how the music is working, of how vertical harmony and horizontal lines progress, provides another point of contact, another window onto what is being memorised.

As previous chapters have stressed, writing imitatively is an excellent route to understanding some of the forces at play in a given musical style. Such an exercise requires you to focus your attention on every instant of sound and silence, probably to a greater degree than you are likely to achieve with any amount of appreciative contemplation of other people's music. Further, since the only effective approach to imitation is by the study of models, this in turn leads you to particularly intensive examination of what you are aiming to reproduce. So, by all means continue to write pastiche, so long as you do not expect the world to have very much use for the fruits of such invention. Begin by expanding outwards chronologically from the Bach-Mozart-Schubert core. Schumann's songs, or those of

Brahms, are not so far from Schubert that some further listening, playing, copying and analysis will not make them accessible. There is a great deal in common between Mozart and his mentor, J.C. Bach, who also wrote keyboard sonatas.

Expand outwards, too, in terms of medium: examine some minuets and slow movements from Mozart's string quartets. They bear enough relationship to the 'core text' piano sonatas to be imitable. Find out how to write for natural horns (from a book such as *Orchestral Technique* by Gordon Jacob, (1940)) and write a sonata exposition for a small classical orchestra of strings and pairs of oboes and horns.

For many, music students, professional and amateur players and listeners alike, the greatest value of an understanding of harmony is in its application as one of the several tools required for making some kind of appreciative analysis of music. So this chapter, while closing the book, also opens the way along various routes towards discovering further how music works.

The amount of musical material available both in print and in recordings is nowadays almost limitless. It may be a sufficiently satisfying experience for some simply to apply the ability to recognise vertical and horizontal harmonic forces at work in particularly striking moments of more and more music heard and played. However, this is only a small part of the total means of appreciation through analysis and dissection. It can be easily expanded by reading some 'formal analyses'*. The intensely subjective 'Essays in Musical Analysis' by Donald Tovey, published from 1935 onwards, still provide a warm and accessible introduction to a considerable corpus of music. Other books deal with specific pieces of repertoire in similarly elegant prose. One of many is *The Beethoven Quartets* by Joseph Kerman (1967). Individual works are sometimes perceptively introduced in this style on the backs of record covers which should not always be spurned as mere 'blurb'.

'Thematic process' analysis, a more objective approach involving the distillation of musical components and the identification of 'prime cells' which grow and are transformed in the composer's mind, was proposed by Rudolph Réti in the 1950s. *The Thematic Process in Music* (1951) was his introduction to the method. *Thematic Patterns in Sonatas of Beethoven* (1967) is a good introduction for pianists who play these sonatas.

Earlier this century, Heinrich Schenker developed a technique designed to throw into relief the 'Fundamental Structure' of a piece. It begins with the concept of extreme compression—a movement of any great tonal work will prove to be the extension in time of no more than a I → V → I progression below a descending three-note line, mediant → supertonic → tonic. It involves a rather daunting system of graphic notation which has been greatly clarified for the English-language reader by *Introduction to Schenkerian Analysis* by Forte and Gilbert (1982), addressed specifically to

---

*The technical term used to differentiate kinds of analysis are borrowed from the long and penetrating article on 'Analysis' by Ian Bent in the *New Grove* dictionary (1980). This article is highly recommended as an introduction to the challenge of further analysis in a variety of methods.

students who have had a year of traditional harmony teaching.

Other analytical methods depend on the identification and manipulation of statistical information. They often result in spectacular graphic, tabular and computer displays which may or may not generate much emotional or aesthetic response to the actual sounds of the music so dissected.

If some understanding of harmony, not just its 'vocabulary' of chords but the 'grammar' which guides their use in extended time, illuminates your listening; if it increases your perception as a performer; if it provides a means of musical discovery, through pastiche; if it serves you as one of the tools of analysis expressed in simple prose or in computer graphics; it will have amply rewarded you for the effort of acquiring it.

Not all of Milton's chains will be untwisted, but enough perhaps to reveal some of the 'hidden strands of harmony'.

Selected Index

This is an extended list of contents rather than a full index. It lists the first or principal appearances of items in the text and is intended to supplement the descriptive chapter headings listed at the beginning of the book. Numerical references are to chapter/paragraph numberings.